Creating the
Champion

"I applaud Molly Kennedy's courage and commitment to help others. Her message about taking charge of your life, regardless of your circumstances, is received loud and clear."

Dave Rozman, National Teen Leadership Conference Director

"Incredible book! An essential and encouraging read for teens, young adults, parents, and educators. Molly presents her unbelievable story with brutal honesty, brings the reader closer with her humor, and then delivers practical strategies to the challenging situations that many of our youth face."

Dr. Ryan S. Schoenfeld, Educational Administrator & Practitioner

"Kennedy's humor and the importance of her story resonate with students, parents, and educators. Her message is powerful and engaging."

Gretchen Cercone, Middle School Principal

"*Creating the Champion Within* addresses the emotional and mental health of young people in a style they understand, need, and respect. If you are going to get one book for your students, this is it."

Jason Cyrek, Health Educator

"Molly's powerful message captivates and inspires teens to want to work toward positive change. This book is a model tool for successful communication on the delicate issues young adults face today."

Amy Ward, M.S., Ed., High School and Middle School Counselor

"It's very rare that I find a book that I believe every young adult should read, but Kennedy captured it with *Creating the Champion Within*. She's funny, she's vulnerable, and she's relatable. It's the book I wish I had in high school, one that talks *to* me, but not at me. Even adults can better communicate with their teen with the tools Molly shares. Don't hesitate to get your copy!"

Kat Hurley, Author of *I Think I'll Make It*

"*Creating the Champion Within* is a must read for anyone who is tired of letting life take the winning medal. Molly's sense of humor and ability to keep it real will inspire you to become better!"

Eliana Reyes, Self-Love Coach & Author of *Purpose: Live it!*

"From cover to cover, this book is on point. For any teen and young adult who is ready to take charge of their life, this is the book to get you there."

Mike Marstellar, Founder of HCM Foundation & Youth Motivational Speaker

Creating the Champion Within

HOW TO GET UP WHEN LIFE KNOCKS YOU DOWN

• • •

Molly Kennedy

Creating the Champion Within
How to Get Up When Life Knocks You Down

By Molly Kennedy

Cover design by Rupa Limbu

Back cover photo by Cathleen Cole

Kennedy, Molly Creating the champion within: how to get up when life knocks you down / by Molly Kennedy. -First edition

Young Adults/Teenagers/Self-Help/Motivation/Resilience/Leadership

Printed in the United States of America

ISBN: 1530729262
ISBN 13: 9781530729265
Library of Congress Control Number: 2016905139
CreateSpace Independent Publishing Platform
North Charleston, South Carolina

For those of you who need a little hope,
things will get better.
I share my story so you can rewrite yours

Contents

Foreword

• • •

WE ARE ALL MOVED AND inspired by many things we come across in life, and this book and the woman who wrote it will be added to your list.

To say you will be inspired and in awe is an understatement when you learn of *true* perseverance in the rawest form. Everyone has a story, everyone has a journey, and everyone has a battle to fight at some point. Yet how often is it that one's story and journey *are* the battle, where it all starts when one is a small child, and the battles are conquered one by one, with little or no assistance, until adulthood?

And how often is one's story, journey, and battle used to do good? To teach? To strengthen others? I guess this is a thread we hear all the time, but I can promise you that this story, this journey, and this battle are unique and profound and amazing—and completely human. You will be a better person after Molly allows you into her life and her lessons. You will be smarter, stronger, and more motivated than before you picked up this book.

—Allison Paull Clement, EdM, MSW, CSW

Author's Note

• • •

THE STORIES AND EXPERIENCES IN this book are based on my personal memories—decades of memories, to be exact. The information is accurate to the best of my knowledge. I have purposely left out the names of people to protect their anonymity.

The successful person has the habit of doing the things failures don't like to do. They don't like doing them either necessarily. But their disliking is subordinated to the strength of their purpose.

—ALBERT E. GRAY

Introduction

• • •

Every July, there I am, watching the ESPYs—ESPN's version of the Academy Awards. Trophies go to the best team, best male and female athlete, and other sports-related categories. On this particular July evening, I am crying my eyes out. Again. Each time I find myself trying to keep my composure, but it's always a sob fest. It could be the Courage Award winner's speech, the replay of Jimmy Valvano's "Never Give Up" speech (which I've heard probably a hundred times), or one of the many stories of athletes who overcame obstacles to reach the highest level in their sport.

My first attempt at writing this book came during one of these meltdowns. I just started typing. I knew that my story was in me and that it had to come out eventually, but I didn't know how or when. I also knew that my vast experiences around athletics had been the making, breaking, and re-making of me.

Sports are very near and dear to my heart. Basketball was my first love. Don't even get me going about NCAA March Madness, especially after the championship game when they always play the video montage to "The Ball Is Tipped"! Oh my God, I can barely breathe through all the snot plugging my nose. How glamorous do I sound right now?

Back to the ESPYs. This annual broadcast is a significant time of reflection for me, an opportunity for me to try to understand a little more each year why I feel so emotionally exhausted, in denial, numb, or perhaps even emotionally bankrupt.

Sports were a survival mechanism for me, a way to express myself that was acceptable and authentically me. Sports allowed me to experience success. They were also the best teacher of so many skills that have allowed me to develop resiliency and become the person I am today and the better version of myself that I strive to be each day.

Creating the Champion Within focuses on the development of the mind-set that's essential to being resilient, successful, happy, and at peace throughout your life.

It's been about five years since I first started writing this book in random chunks at ESPY time. I have known for some time that I wanted to write a book for teens and young adults, and it's because of some truly unfortunate circumstances that I have finally reached the point where I am emotionally and mentally ready to write this. Even as an old lady, I am still learning to appreciate all the garbage that life threw my way—and there have been truckloads of it. All the bad stuff ends up being the best teacher, because what you learn in the difficult moments has the potential to shape you into an amazing human being *if* you choose that path.

I'm so happy to be able to share this book with you. The goal is to take you on your own personal journey as I share some of my experiences and stories and for you to explore how you can relate them to your life. This book will also help you learn from my many mistakes to save you years and tears. Another goal is to help you feel energized and empowered to take full control of your thoughts, words, and actions and to create the life you desire and deserve.

I promise that the stories I share are not just to hear myself talk—well, type. They each have a purpose and a lesson to teach. I am definitely not going to tell you what to do. You have plenty of adults already doing that. The best way I know to make a point or help you see things from a new perspective is to share my experiences through stories. You can use the lessons to make fewer mistakes than I did and to become happier a lot sooner than I did.

My initial purpose in writing this book was to help you realize that you are capable of overcoming any obstacle that life throws your way. Plenty of obstacles will be in your path. That's a guarantee! I strongly suggest that you face these obstacles head-on *as soon as possible*, or else they will haunt you until you resolve their many-layered, vise-grip effect.

Trust me; I was a hot mess for a long time because I did not face my problems until I was an adult. As of this writing, I'm still working on some issues. Life is a process. It's not about being perfect. It's about doing and being your best each day. Some days, your best is amazeballs! Some days, your best is about making it through without hurting everyone in your path.

I am asking you to *interact* with this book. Simply reading is nice, but when you fully engage and participate in the reading, this allows you to take away more and put the concepts into action in your own life. Wishing, wanting, and hoping are fine, but to truly make changes and improvements, you must take action.

The end of each chapter will include a section called "Your Turn," where I invite you to take the time to write your answers down. Go at your own pace. If you get stuck, come back to the questions later. Grab an extra sheet of paper or a journal if that helps. Remember, *action* is the key to taking control of your life and being successful.

As you read this book, I encourage you to put it down and genuinely reflect on how the stories and experiences I share relate to what you have experienced or are currently experiencing. I'm not calling this a self-help book but more of a self-guided tour to your awesomeness. You're welcome.

If you don't apply what you learn from these pages, I will hunt you down and slap you upside your head. I'm kidding. I'll throw a forearm shiver. Sorry, it's the result of watching way too much WWF growing up. (Yes, WWF, because WWE didn't exist yet. I feel old.)

Sometimes I use funny violence to make a point. My point here? Stop making excuses, blaming others, acting like the victim (even if you are one), and giving away your power. Life will knock you down repeatedly. The key is to get back up each time. It is time to take charge of your life and create the champion within!

It's game time, so get your game face on. Let's do this!

CHAPTER 1

Take Back Your Power

• • •

I HAVE SOME GOOD NEWS and some bad news. Ready? Here it is.

You are in complete control of your future.

That's bad news if you often make excuses and give away your power, act like a victim of anything and everything, or act as if you can't be held accountable for your thoughts, words, and choices. This is bad news if you often say things such as, "She made me so mad." That can begin to change today if you choose.

You are in complete control of your future.

That's good news if you are ready to acknowledge your weaknesses, appreciate your strengths, and accept the freedom and responsibility that come with young adulthood. When you create the champion within, it means you are taking control of your mind-set. When you control that, you take charge of your life.

I'm sure you are at a point in your life where you are maturing and craving more freedom and responsibility. As you get older, it's really important to be in control of your thoughts, words, and actions.

Let's look at a hypothetical scenario to wrap your head around how this mind-set thing works. Hint: what you see is what you get. Brace yourself.

Do you have an annoying sibling who lives at home with you? I'll play the odds and go with yes.

If your mind-set says, "My sister is annoying," you will find every piece of evidence to support your belief. You'll look at her and say, "Ugh! She is so annoying. Look at her…breathing."

I mean, she could solve world hunger and be celebrated around the globe as a hero, but you'd say, "Um, hi, World. Here's the thing about your hero. I don't know if you know this, but when we were in high school, she would barge into my room. She didn't knock, and I had a sign on the door that said 'knock first.' She came in and took my hoodie without asking. And when she returned it, it was dirty. So how do you like your hero now, World?"

And the world would say, "Um, we love her because she solved world hunger."

And you'd say, "Hashtag, she took my hoodie."

And the world would say, "Hashtag, flip your 20."

Your mind-set is so warped that you can't see beyond the negative filter you have of your sister and recognize the good she did. Your opinion and perspective are so blurry that you are in a headspace to find only her faults.

This is how it works in *every* situation. What you see is what you get.

I bet you're wondering, "Molly, what is flip your 20?" Let me explain with some context.

The foundation of creating the champion within revolves around the concept of your paradigm. Understanding and applying this will help you create the life you want. It's really important!

Paradigm is a weird-looking word. On paper, it looks like *pair-a-dig-em*. The correct pronunciation is "pair-a-dime." So I call it *20 Cent*. I'll give you a moment to let it sink in. I'm patient; I'll wait. I'm going to grab a glass of water while you figure it out.

OK, my friends, my thirst is quenched. In case you are still confused, a pair of dimes equals twenty cents. I'm pseudogangsta, so I call it 20 Cent. I'm sure you know the rapper 50 Cent.

"Hey, shorty. It's your birthday, and we're gonna party like it's your birthday."

You got 50. I'm an old lady, so I got 20.

Are you thinking I'm a little less *gangsta* and a whole lot more *gangster*? You're smart.

Your paradigm (now called 20 Cent) is your opinion, your point of view, and your perspective. It is a self-fulfilling prophecy. What you see is what you get. It's like the filter through which you see the world.

Just as on social media, you have your favorite and least favorite filters. You want to either highlight or hide some part of the picture. Your 20 Cent works the exact same way. You can choose a positive or negative filter for the day. It is always your choice.

I am sure you've heard the fancy people say that it's important to have a paradigm shift to see things from a new perspective. This is true. However,

I am not fancy, so instead of saying paradigm shift, I say, "Flip your 20!" See what I did there?

The beauty of your 20 Cent (i.e., your filter) is that it exists in only one place: your mind. More specifically, it's your mind-set. Your 20 Cent works as shown in Disney Pixar's *Inside Out.* We each have all those little voices in our head (joy, anger, sadness, fear, and disgust). They show up at different times and around different people and determine how we react. In turn, they determine how our day will go. It's all inside your head.

To clarify, *20 Cent* and *filter* are synonyms, and I will use them interchangeably. You are the only one in absolute control over it. Nobody has the ability to make you think or feel anything. You are in ultimate control of your thoughts, feelings, words, and actions. That is powerful. Take back your power.

Sadly, we give our power away all the time by blaming others and letting them push our buttons. Then they are stuck in our minds, and they own us. You can't shake how annoyed you are with them. Am I striking a cord here?

This is how it works in every situation.

For example, if you believe your teacher hates you, you're right. No, seriously. Teachers take an oath, just like doctors. The doctor's Hippocratic Oath is, in part, "Above all else, do no harm." The teacher's oath before he or she can step into a classroom with students is, "I, [state your name], promise to hate all my students." That's why you feel like that sometimes. It's federal law. Don't hate the player—hate the game.

Almost the entire previous paragraph is a lie. As a former teacher, we don't take an oath. The good news is your teachers probably don't hate you. The reality is, if you think they hate you, that's your fault. Yep, I said it. Only *you* can change your filter of that teacher, that class, or any situation.

Your 20 Cent takes place in your brain. Because you are the only one who lives up there, you are the only one who controls it. That means you are literally the only one who controls your thoughts, words, and actions. I have repeated this concept on purpose. It's that important.

Of course, that also means you can no longer blame anybody else for how you feel. You are certainly allowed to feel all the emotions out there. I encourage you to do so and to take responsibility for them. Your 20 Cent is based on your mood, past experiences, beliefs, relationships, and so on.

It works like this in every situation. I'll share one more example to make sure I have clearly explained 20 Cent.

Think about a time when you were watching a scary movie with some friends. At the scariest moments, chances are that some friends screamed in terror, while others barely flinched or maybe even laughed. You all witnessed the same scene in the same environment, yet your reactions were markedly different.

Let's examine this for a moment. If I had been there watching, I would have not only screamed but maybe even peed a little bit, too. I don't watch scary movies, because my filter is "I'm a huge scaredy-cat." What I see is what I get. I believe I'm a scaredy-cat, so I think and act like one.

Perhaps it started when the movie *Halloween* was first shown on TV. My older siblings (I'm the youngest of six) thought it was a good idea to have me watch it. I was pretty young. It totally freaked me out. I began to think the boogeyman was living under my bed. To make sure he didn't grab my feet, I would pretend I was a WWF wrestler. I would turn off the light near the door, run past my sister's bed, and fly in the air like Jimmy "Superfly" Snuka (Google him) off the top ropes, dropping an elbow on my pillow. See, the boogeyman couldn't grab my feet and pull me under the bed if I were flying through the air. I was smart like that.

Or perhaps I'm a scaredy-cat because my siblings would tie string to my bedroom doorknob and pull it closed when I was lying in bed. They pretended it was a ghost.

These experiences shaped my 20 Cent of the dark, and I became afraid of it. I'm a little bit better as an adult and am not *as* afraid of the dark (I couldn't sleep with the closet door open until my late twenties). But I still don't watch scary movies. That's my filter, and it's not important enough for me to want to change it, so I don't.

Fortunately, this limiting filter doesn't affect my quality of life. However, I have had plenty of negative and limiting filters that have affected it. I'm confident you do, too. I didn't start working on them until I was in my thirties. Please don't make this same mistake! #flipyour20

Let's revisit the "my teacher hates me" 20 Cent. If you walk into that class each time with a limiting or negative filter, you are creating an instant disadvantage for yourself. If your perspective is that your teacher hates you, then you automatically put up a wall, which in turn means you will likely be unable to learn at your full potential. You sit there and think, "If she hates me, then I'm going to hate her."

Your disdain for your teacher (which you have created) is a limiting 20 Cent. You will be distracted by your thoughts of not liking her and finding evidence to prove how unfair she is. As a result, you won't be focusing on the material that is your responsibility to learn.

Here's some good news. Each time you walk into the class, you can choose a new filter. You can choose to believe that your belief of your teacher hating you stemmed from one or two rough encounters at the beginning of the semester. You know that excelling in that class will help you punch your ticket to graduation. This is a big deal, because your education is your ticket to wherever you want to go in life.

Knowing this, you can choose to say "Good morning" when you enter class. It's better than growling at her as you usually do. You leave her wondering, "Did he just growl at me? Is he a bear now or just emo?"

I bet you're chuckling right now because you have done that before. Again, as a former teacher, I'm pulling from firsthand experience.

You can choose to stop slouching in class, looking as if you got shot with a poisonous blow dart. Instead, you can choose to sit up. Instead of rolling your eyes at your teacher, you can choose to make regular eye contact. Instead of being a disruption in class, you can choose to raise your hand and participate at least once every class.

I'm a realist. Please understand that I'm not saying you need to skip into school while singing the show tune "I Love to Come to School." Dude, don't do that! You'll have no friends.

Your 20 Cent has another layer. Your filter is like a song that you have playing over and over in your head all day long. When you are in a good mood and your filter is positive, it's as if your favorite song is on repeat. You're jamming out. Your self-talk is probably something like, "I'm talented, compassionate, artistic, athletic," and so on. You'll play those thoughts all day long. Even if people around you are being jerks, you are going to have a good day because you choose to have an awesome mind-set for the day.

What's your favorite song? What's the song that puts you in an amazing mood no matter what mood you start with? For me, it's "I Choose" by India. Arie. I sing that song so loud in my car. Fortunately, no one can hear me. My singing voice is not my greatest strength. People's ears have been known to bleed upon hearing me sing.

On days when every little thing annoys you, your self-talk is probably something like, "I'm ugly. No one likes me. I'm not smart enough. I'm worthless." A comment your friend said yesterday was fine, but today you snap at him. You know those days, right?

A negative filter can feel like your least favorite song playing in your head all day long. Let's be honest; you would delete or skip that song. No way would it play continuously. You would be annoyed and agitated and do whatever you had to do to not listen to it anymore.

What's your least favorite song? For me, it's Rihanna's "Diamonds." I actually think the words are good, but her voice when she belts out "shine bright like a diamond" is nails on a chalkboard to me. Again, I am no music aficionado. But I know I want to rip my face off when I hear that part of the song. I get angry. Note: She doesn't *make* me angry. That's *my* choice.

You would never play your least favorite song repeatedly. This brings us to a potentially harmful aspect of your 20 Cent.

Think about how many times you've taken someone's negative comments about you or actions toward you and played them on a loop in your head. The danger with this is that when you hear something long enough, you start to believe it.

This happens when somebody says a rude comment to you or about you.

- "You're a loser."
- "Nobody likes you."
- "Why can't you be more like your brother/sister?"
- "You'll never figure it out."
- "You're stupid."
- "You're a waste of my time."
- "You're not as great as you think you are."
- "You're ugly."
- "No one from this neighborhood ever goes anywhere in life."
- "We don't have enough money for you to go to college."
- "You'll never amount to anything."
- "You might as well give up on that dream now."
- Add your own here.

These examples are simply someone's 20 Cent of you. *Just because somebody says something doesn't mean it's true.*

What do you do with those comments? Be honest with yourself here. I bet that many times you take the comment and internalize it, especially if it is said repeatedly, convincingly, or by someone who is supposed to be on your side. When you hear something long enough, you start to believe it. You have taken *their* comment—*their* filter—and made it your negative soundtrack, because that is all you play in your head all day long. You gave them your power. Today is the day when this stops!

Pause. Think how many times you have given your power to someone else and said, "He ruined my day." Truth be told, he didn't ruin your day. He said something, and you chose to interpret it in a way that struck a chord with you. You took it to heart. You took it personally. Now you have allowed your day to be ruined.

Stop blaming others for how you feel. I am guilty of doing this a lot throughout my life. It's a waste of energy and a certain route to being unhappy.

When they get in your head, they own you. You gave away all your power, probably because you didn't know you had any power. Every single one of you has a great power: the power to choose how you think, feel, and act. That's all you. Your mind-set is prime real estate. Stop letting people live in the penthouse when they aren't paying rent!

Somebody's opinion of you doesn't have to become your reality. Yes, everybody has the right to his or her opinion. But only you can give people's opinions any power or meaning. You choose what you give power to. One of my favorite quotes is from Eleanor Roosevelt: "Nobody can make you feel inferior without your consent." This encapsulates flip your 20. You choose.

Your Turn

1. Identify one time you believed some of the negative things someone said about you and let that person ruin your day. Who was it? What did the person say or do? How did it negatively affect you?

_____

_____

_____

2. What you see is what you get. Identify a time when you "got" exactly what you "saw." Give one positive and one negative example.

Positive: _____

_____

Negative: _____

_____

3. What's your 20 Cent of your
   a. home life?

   _____

   _____

   b. academic future?

   _____

   _____

   c. friendships?

   _____

   _____

d. attitude?

_____

_____

e. sports/music/extracurricular abilities?

_____

_____

4. Pick one item from question 3 that you want to improve. How will you improve it?

_____

_____

_____

CHAPTER 2

We've All Got "Stuff"

• • •

EVERY SINGLE HUMAN BEING, DEAD or alive, has had to deal with bad, unfortunate, and unfair circumstances in his or her life. Every single human being. I call those unfair and bad things "stuff."

Look, we all have stuff. You're undoubtedly thinking about *your* stuff right now.

Take a moment to scan the list. Do you see any of your stuff here?

Bullying
Abuse
Abandonment
Addiction in family
Unfair treatment
Suicidal thoughts
Living away from home
Learning disability
Being told you are worthless
Poor support network
Feeling isolated
Rough neighborhood
Always being compared to others
Unrealistic expectations of others

Neglect
Anger issues
Divorce
Loss of loved one
Depression
Suicidal actions
Not living with relatives
Lacking social skills
Trauma
Self-harm
No guidance from adults
Low self-esteem

Maybe I'm a mind reader. I'm guessing you're thinking, "She can't possibly guess what I'm thinking right now." Am I right? I know.

Even if I weren't a mind reader, I would use this same list. Everybody has stuff. Even someone who looks as if he or she has it all together and has a perfect life has stuff. To be clear, nobody's life is perfect. Perfection is *not* a human quality. Everybody walks around with struggles regardless of what it looks like on the outside. Everybody has a story.

Most of this stuff is stuff that others put into your life without your permission. Regardless of who put it there or the reasons it's there, it's there. It may not be your fault that it's there, but it *is* your responsibility how you handle it. You can either give up or get up. Your choice.

Most teens are dealing with more than one thing on this list. When I travel around the country speaking, teens always come up to me afterward, and I often hear, "I'm dealing with multiple things on that list. And it's tough. I thought I was the only one, so I haven't talked about it."

Having stuff does not make you unique.

Thriving despite it, does.

Regardless of what stuff you're dealing with, you can persevere, be stronger, be resilient, and be better off—if you choose to. It's a choice. It's a mind-set.

I am proof of this. Here's my stuff: My parents divorced when I was about one. My mother was an alcoholic and wasn't around much, which means my grandparents came over to make sure we kids were fed and bathed. My mother remarried an abusive man who almost choked my oldest brother to death on the stairs (I was eight years old, and my brother's boot-scuff marks remained on the wall after his struggle.) She stayed with him. I had an eating disorder in high school. I was suicidal in my teens and had those thoughts deep into my twenties. I was abused, abandoned, and neglected. I ran away at fifteen and never went back. So, technically, I'm a runaway.

I remember feeling as if hope had run out when I was fifteen. My grandma came up to me and said in a snotty tone, "What's this I hear about you wanting to kill yourself? Don't be ridiculous. Now, go wash your hands and get ready for supper." It was never addressed again. That's basically the biggest cry for help someone can give, and I was ignored. Remember what I said about your 20 Cent? If you hear something long enough, you start to believe it. I was starting to believe I didn't matter.

Less than two months after I ran away from home, I received a letter from my mom's lawyer. I still have a copy. It says, "My client is no longer responsible for Molly's upkeep and maintenance." Upkeep and maintenance made me feel like a dog. My mother never came to get me. I went to the same school until I graduated. She lived a couple miles away from my school, yet she didn't want me. All she had to do was come to school and say, "My daughter, Molly Kennedy, has run away from home. I don't know where she is. Is she here? It's time for her to come home." She didn't do that. It was hard to wrap my head around my mom not wanting me and how quickly she gave up on me. I really believed that I didn't matter and that I was a piece of garbage.

I'm a fan of honesty. So I need to let you know that I did have a typical teenage-girl attitude. I cannot deny that. I was an angry teen.

But I wasn't a bad kid or anything. I wasn't engaging in criminal activity or doing drugs. I bet I was probably a lot like you. You go to school, go to your extracurricular activities, and pretty much do what you're supposed to do, for the most part. You are a normal human being until you get home. When your parents ask, "How was your day?" you turn into a demonic monster, hissing and yelling, "Leave me alone! Nobody understands me!" If you're smiling right now, you're admitting guilt. It's OK. We've all been there. You're not alone.

You know *those My Super Sweet 16* shows on TV where the teen gets a BMW? Those shows are crazy and not realistic for the average teen.

I remember my sweet-sixteen gift. It was a big, blue duffel bag, and all my belongings fit in it. I was homeless at this point. I was going back and forth between friends' houses, my grandparents' house, and a teacher's house.

Finally, I found a permanent place to live. I moved in with a well-respected member of my school community and her family. She had a husband and children. My friends and I had babysat their kids before. I remember giving her a Mother's Day card that said, "You're like a mother to me." She helped me get control over my anorexia before it got out of control. She gave me a safe, secure place to live. She provided food, shelter, and clothing. And it was so great, because I finally believed that I had my first real, trusted adult who genuinely cared about me.

I remember thinking how lucky I was, because I knew that this stuff was not how my life was supposed to turn out. In my gut, I knew that I would accomplish cool things and that my life had to get better at some point. I continued to immerse myself in school, sports, and anything related to fitness and health. It was my way of setting myself apart from my family. I rebelled against my family by being smart, athletic, and fit.

After dealing with all that stuff, I remember thinking that everything would finally change.

I was right. It did change.

That's when she began abusing me. When I say *abusing*, I mean that the person I looked up to and trusted the most in the world molested (sexually abused) me more times than I can count. As if this weren't bad enough, because she was more like a mother to me, it had an incest feel to it. It was so perverted. She gave me alcohol as a teen and molested me. She took me across state lines and molested me. I felt like an unlovable, worthless piece of trash. When you're told something long enough, you start to believe it.

I wish I'd known how to flip my 20 back then.

I didn't tell anybody what was happening. From the outside it looked like everything was great. She was applauded by those who knew I lived with her. Those people thought she saved me. In my weak, twisted mind, I think I did, too.

Enduring the abuse almost seemed as if it were my payment for food, clothes, shelter, staying at the same school, and playing sports. My cost was her hurting me in any way she wanted. She knew my mom didn't want me. She knew I wasn't going to be able to live with my grandparents. I didn't feel like I had any options at that time. Any attention is better than zero attention.

She then began to isolate me even further from my friends. She didn't live close to my school, so it was hard to have access to my old neighborhood and peers.

I felt like she had destroyed me, destroyed my soul. It forever altered my life, affecting my ability to trust, to have healthy emotions, and to have healthy relationships. It took me almost twenty years to begin to recover, because that's how long I stuffed that secret and most of my other stuff way down.

I don't want you to waste twenty years—let alone twenty minutes—because of your stuff. With the right mind-set and help, you can persevere and thrive despite your stuff. I wouldn't say that if I didn't believe it. I promise.

Sharing my stuff with you isn't easy, but it is important. I share it because life's challenges are not supposed to paralyze you; they are there to help you discover who you are. The struggle is part of the journey. I wasted twenty years being angry and miserable and hurting a lot of people along the way. Learn from my mistakes. Your choices are on you. No more excuses!

We all have stuff. Yours may be different from mine, but we all have it. Maybe your mom didn't abandon you, but you've felt left out or ignored. Maybe you've never been abused, but you've been hurt by someone and didn't understand why. Maybe for you, your stuff is about being smothered by the expectations and stress of always needing to excel. Maybe you're always being compared to your sibling. We all have stuff, even the adults in your life. Nobody gets through life unscathed.

LIFE-CHANGING ALERT (insert siren sound here): This next section is a game changer. Read carefully.

When somebody is mean, rude, or nasty to you, *it's not about you.*

It's about them.

You are simply the **unfortunate target** of the stuff they haven't dealt with yet.

Reread the last three sentences as many times as necessary. Put it as a screen saver on your phone and laptop. Post it on your mirror. Get it tattooed to your forehead backward so that when you look in the mirror, you can read it. (Just kidding about the tattoo part, of course.)

This is a life-changing concept because we have a tendency to take everything so personally, especially as teens.

For example, maybe your dad has been really mean to you lately by calling you names and has been in your face from the time you get home until the time you leave for school the next day. That doesn't feel good. Then you come to school frustrated, hurt, and not with the right mind-set to learn. As a result, you don't pay attention in class, you argue with your first-period teacher, and you let your grades drop. It's a snowball effect. Yikes!

But you have the choice to think, "This stinks, but it's not about me. I know my dad's been frustrated at his job, that his boss is a jerk to him, and that I'm the unfortunate target of his frustration."

Acknowledging this will not make it stop or make you happy that it's happening. I wouldn't insult your intelligence like that.

If you acknowledge this, however, it gives you permission to talk to a trusted adult at home or at school who will listen to you and provide tips and strategies on how to handle your feelings in a more productive way.

When I was teaching, I can assure you that I always preferred that students tell me about their problems, which always had a direct effect on their negative behavior. When we as teachers know the problem, we can do something about it. We can address the problem directly, diffuse our daily first-period battle, and get you back on the road to being successful and happy. But you have to believe this "unfortunate target" thing and tell an adult you trust.

I've been on both sides of this coin.

Remember when I told you my grandma didn't get me help when I was a desperate teen? At the time, I interpreted it as she didn't love me, as if she didn't care if I hurt myself. It took me two decades to wrap my head around the reality of that situation.

I knew she loved me and my siblings. When we were younger and my mom was out drinking, my grandma would come over and make sure we were fed and bathed. She made sure we had winter boots, gloves, and coats. She loved us.

My grandma was born in 1919. She survived the Great Depression. She also survived my grandpa being severely injured in World War II and being in recovery for three years before he returned home. She did this while she was working and taking care of my mom, who was less than four years old at the time.

These circumstances hardened her. She was a tough woman, and being all lovey-dovey wasn't her thing as we got older. I finally realized twenty years later that I was simply the unfortunate target of her being hardened and shaped by her life experiences. It wasn't about me. I took it personally, which negatively shaped my 20 Cent. I wish I'd known better back then.

Understanding this now will help you as you deal with the negative words and actions that people throw your way. Whether they are loved ones or strangers, *it's not about you.* I'm not saying that being aware of this will suddenly make it extremely easy to handle. I am saying that this knowledge can prevent you from taking it personally so that it doesn't negatively affect you more than it needs to.

I've been on the other side of this coin as well. When I was teaching, I worked with one of the nicest guys I have ever met. We taught the same subject and grade levels. However, he became the unfortunate target of my stuff that I hadn't dealt with. To add insult to injury, it got even worse during my unraveling.

I was still wearing my tough-girl mask yet dying on the inside. To save face, I had to puff up and make myself feel better. I would be aggressive in seeking to get my way on many decisions that should have involved a compromise. I would show the tough-girl side enough to get my way, to prove to myself that I was worthy after so many years of being shown the opposite. And I was a total control freak. Seriously, it was bad! I would volunteer to type up most of the new documents, tests, and projects because I knew I could do it my way—the right way. On many days, I was a nightmare to work with.

During the height of my unraveling at work, I would lock myself in my classroom and turn the lights off so that I wouldn't be bothered or have to talk to anyone. When I'm in a really bad state of mind, I'm at my absolute worst. It's best not to come near me. Just leave me alone.

But my extra-nice colleague was always trying to help, be kind, and make sure I was OK. During one of my worst days—lights off, door locked—I heard the jingling of keys at my door. It was him, unlocking my door and about to come in. My body got warm, and my mind was about to break. I don't remember if I even let him get a foot or a word in before I snapped at him in a terribly nasty tone, "Are you kidding me right now?"

He closed the door and left. I wanted to be left alone. The sad part is, he was trying to be there for me, but I was so deep in my own stuff that I didn't know how to receive his kindness. Being on the receiving end of kindness was a foreign concept to me. How sad and pathetic is that?

I knew how to be hurt, taken advantage of, and manipulated. I knew that if someone was doing something nice for me, strings were always attached, and I would have to pay up sooner or later. I had been in survival mode for so long with my walls up, keeping others at bay, that I didn't know how to recognize genuine kindness. I was too hurt and angry to see it, even when it was literally right in front of my face.

I'm not proud of those actions, but they are part of my story. We have to own our stories in order to move forward and write the next chapters with our own words.

Your Turn

1. What are the top three items on your stuff list that you need to address and begin to heal from? What will be your first step for each?

   a. _____

   _____

   b. _____

   _____

   c. _____

   _____

2. Whose stuff are you the unfortunate target of? How does this affect you? How can you change how you let it affect you?

   _____

   _____

   _____

3. Who is the unfortunate target of your stuff? Does it require an apology? How will you take action to stop taking it out on others?

   _____

   _____

   _____

CHAPTER 3

Take Off Your Mask

• • •

Do you let the negative actions of others get to you and bring you down? Do you react by trying to act tough and save face? Do you put up the wall and act all tough and angry? Or do you put on the happy, smiling guy or girl mask, pretending everything is fine?

Take off your mask.

All that your tough-guy or tough-girl mask or attitude does is show others that you are hurting. You reveal the hurt when you walk around with an angry expression for no reason, are quick to jump all over someone's case, or act so tough as if you don't need any help. You show your hurt when you have the attitude of people better butt out of your business, or else.

There's a problem with that angry mask. The tougher and angrier you act, the more hurt you are inside. People who are hurt end up hurting people. I may have just blown your cover. Sorry, not sorry.

Get it out. Talk it out. Because you act out what you don't talk out, and that never turns out good. It usually involves alcohol, drugs, violence, isolation, bullying, self-harm, and so on. Please don't make the same mistakes I did by cramming all the bad stuff down and covering up your pain with your mask. Take off your mask.

I used to think that asking for help was weak. I was wrong for over twenty years. My mask got so thick that I started to believe that was who I was. I got lost behind my mask. And I didn't let anyone truly *know* me.

I remember speaking at a middle-school assembly. The principal contacted me a few days later. She said that after the assembly, a student told the school counselor that his mom was abusing him. The police officer asked what had made him come forward now, for the abuse had been happening for some time.

He said, "We had an assembly at school this week, and I realized it wasn't my fault and I deserved better." He chose to have the courage to stand up to his mom and say, "Mom, it's not OK for you to hurt me anymore." That boy decided he was valuable and didn't deserve to be hurt. He got help and has forever changed the course of his life. He didn't have to wear the "everything is fine" mask anymore. That is pure #flipyour20.

Do you wear the happy, smiling mask? You know the one, where you walk around acting as if everything is great, fine, and perfect. After all, you are a member of the National Honor Society, class president, captain of the team, first chair in orchestra, and a community volunteer. I mean, what could possibly be wrong with your life?

You know the answer to that, because when you go home and take off your smiley mask, you're sad or hurting. But people perceive that you're such a great kid, never in trouble, and a high flyer. Your 20 Cent is dangerous, because you think you have to be perfect and don't want to let anyone down. Yet perfection is not a human quality. Strive for excellence, yes, but not perfection. You, too, are allowed to have problems and turn to a trusted adult who can help you. You deserve that.

I have some street cred here as a recovering perfectionist. You are human, and you have flaws. That's OK. Learn to embrace this, because it will save you a lot of stress and disappointment. Take off your mask.

Think about the people in your life you give your power to. Be honest with yourself. It can be tough, because you're at the beginning of this awesome journey of being in control of your life and your future. Taking away the security blanket of blaming, making excuses, and wearing the mask is tough. It's also a skill that takes lots of practice and lots of patience.

Here's an insider tip: many adults do not do what I am asking you to do. So you may not be used to seeing this new concept of #flipyour20.

I can ask you to try this because I have done it myself. I will never ask you to do anything I haven't done. I think that's fair.

OK, I'll go first. I gave my power to *so many* people. As a result, my mask got thicker and thicker so that I could protect myself. In reality, I was hurting myself and didn't realize it until many years later. I gave my power away to two of my former administrators when I was still teaching. Two significant events occurred, and the administrators didn't support me and went back on their word. This was a dagger in my heart, and it brought me to my knees with hatred, betrayal, and disdain. There's always a reason why things get us fired up. Our reactions are not accidental. They are in direct proportion to how we deal with our stuff. Our reactions are 100 percent controllable.

I'd like to share the first of these significant events here. I'll save the second event for chapter 4.

EVENT ONE: CRAZY

Long story short (sort of), I was teaching at a high school and coaching JV girls' basketball. Sometimes we had practice in the middle-school gym, which was two blocks behind the high school. The modified team practiced before us, and their female coach was out short-term because of health reasons. A young male coach was filling in for a few weeks. On this particular evening, he left the building before all his players left the locker room, which is against policy.

My team started to warm up in the gym. I told the three remaining modified players that they needed to leave because their coach was gone. I was not responsible for them, and I needed to lock things up so that I could start my practice.

Their attitude came out immediately. Wow, were they disrespectful and nasty! This was not how students talked to teachers and certainly not how I was used to being spoken to. So I got more and more stern about them needing to leave. They wouldn't leave and were moving ridiculously slow. They were making disrespectful comments, rolling their eyes, and lip smacking the whole time. I definitely raised my voice, entering the locker room and yelling for them to get out. I said or yelled, "Get out!" a number of times.

Finally, they left. We started practice. Ten minutes later, we heard pounding on the wooden gym doors. Then the pounding moved to the locker-room-hallway door, which was glass. I could see those same three girls and a woman. The woman looked angry as she kept pounding on the glass. I was surprised it didn't shatter. The pounding stopped, and we kept practicing. Then I heard that glass door unlock.

Uh-oh. I knew in my gut (FYI, trust your gut instinct; it's usually right) that something bad was coming. I went into self-preservation mode, like when a computer powers down. You know that whooshing sound it makes? I did that internally to go void of all emotions.

In a flash, this crazy woman stormed at me and confronted me, eye to eye. I noticed she was wearing lovely, green contacts. She was so close to me that I could see her pores. I didn't move. I could see my girls (I call all my athletes "my girls") in the background, and my ultimate goal was to keep them safe. I also took being a good role model very seriously and wanted to teach them how to be calm and not instantly retaliate to save face.

I should mention at this time that my reputation was along the lines of, "Miss Kennedy is funny but strict. She's cool, but don't mess with her. She could probably beat up everybody in this school, including the male students and male teachers." It became a larger-than-life caricature of how tough I was. I have to admit, I was partly responsible for this image. I'd wear my Incredible Hulk T-shirt and ask if the students liked my self-portrait on it. I did this in part to protect myself from all the damage and stuff I had endured earlier in life but hadn't yet dealt with. Acting tough and keeping people away equals keeping me safe. But this tough thing ended up getting out of control and having a life of its own.

The crazy woman started swearing at me and accusing me of hitting her daughter, who was one of the girls from the locker room. In a monotone voice, I repeated that I hadn't hit her and that she and the others wouldn't leave when I'd repeatedly asked. The woman was already full-throttle crazy. It didn't matter what I said. She repeatedly accused me of hitting her daughter, and she swore up one side and down the other. This went on for a few minutes. It was scary.

Then she dropped her purse. In case you don't know why this is significant, let me enlighten you. When a woman is angry and drops her purse, takes her earrings out, or takes off her heels, you should run, because something really bad is about to go down. And it did.

She raised her hands to my shoulders, hauled off, and shoved me backward. I stumbled a few feet. My head whipped back. And I stood steady in my new position. She came at me again, nose to nose. She was cursing me out and probably shocked that I didn't hit her back. I needed to keep my girls safe, especially with the three locker-room girls cheering on the woman. They were literally cheering her on and encouraging her to "get me." She wasn't going to get the lawsuit she had hoped for by expecting me to retaliate. No dice, Crazy! You're messing with one of the most self-disciplined people you will ever meet. Sorry, but not really.

I called a couple of my girls over to grab their phones and call 911. I was happy to keep Crazy nose to nose to keep her away from them. One of my girls started dialing, and Crazy said to her, "Ain't nobody calling the [darn] cops. Hang up." My player was so scared that she hung up. I restated, in a monotone voice, "Call 911 and tell them where we are and that your coach is being physically assaulted by an intruder."

A different girl called and started to talk to the 911 dispatcher, and then she gave the phone to me. As I started talking to the police, Crazy and the three girls ran away. They literally ran away. It looked like a scene from the TV show *Cops*: "Bad boys, bad boys, whatcha gonna do?" They returned quickly to grab their purses and bags, laughing the whole time.

After meeting the police in the hallway and giving them my story, I came back into the gym and saw the coolest thing: my girls were running the next drill on their own, being focused and productive. They were awesome! I was so fortunate to coach great girls. I let them finish the drill, not saying much. My hands were literally shaking from the adrenaline rush. I called my girls over to debrief. Most of them had never experienced such a scary event before.

One of the major lessons learned was that saving face does not mean fighting back. Being tough and strong does not equal being violent. Again, I had a reputation of being tough and able to beat up anybody, even though I'm a nonviolent person. I always say, "I'm not violent. I just look like I am." But I love my muscles and will not apologize for them. Being tough is having self-discipline, self-control, and integrity. Strength is practicing what you preach, putting the welfare of others before your own, and being a role model. That's tough.

Retaliating and hitting the crazy woman would have shown tremendous weakness in that split second. We all have the right to self-defense, but in that moment, I did the right thing. *The right thing isn't always the easy thing. But it is always the right thing.* Understand, many times since then, I've visualized beating her face in until all her teeth fly out. I imagined it, but I *did not act on it.* That's the difference.

The initial phase of being let down by the administrators and knowing that I was pretty much on my own happened in the next few days. One administrator said that he was glad I wasn't hurt and that I had the right to defend myself. That was great to hear. But after that, most of the comments from administrators were more along the lines of the following:

* "Our money is on you."
* "You would have destroyed her."
* "She's one lucky woman that you didn't retaliate."
* "You would have kicked her butt."

Besides the one administrator, I didn't hear anything from the others along the lines of the following:

* "Thank you."
* "Thank you for putting yourself in the line of danger to keep your girls safe."
* "Thank you for being a good role model."
* "Thank you for saving the district a massive lawsuit."

The only people who responded appropriately with concern and gratitude were some of the parents of my girls. I truly appreciated that.

I ended up getting a restraining order against Crazy. She couldn't come within so many feet of me. She couldn't come to my workplace or near my home. I wouldn't have to deal with her or her daughter until September when the girl entered high school.

The next school year came. I spoke with the counselors to make sure the daughter of Crazy wasn't in my class or near my room, as much as possible. All was going well until open-house night in the fall of her freshman year. I was standing outside my classroom when Crazy turned the corner. We locked eyes. She turned and went the other way. I gathered all the sign-in sheets as proof that she was there. She was breaking the restraining order, which was grounds for being arrested.

I contacted the police the next day and informed my administration of the new developments. The police went to arrest her at her house, and she pulled out a different, updated restraining order that allowed her to come to my workplace. What? The court had never informed me of this, which is my legal right. I requested to have a court appearance in front of the judge, with Crazy and her obnoxious attorney. I knew that the restraining order was a couple of months from expiring and wouldn't go back to its original restrictions. However, it was important for me to advocate for myself and my safety. I knew Crazy. I'd seen Crazy. She scared me.

You always have a voice, and you always have the right to stand up for yourself in a dignified manner. Please remember that. Your voice matters.

The problem of giving away my power—my 20 Cent—began here. Because Crazy now had the legal right to be in my workplace, I asked the principal for the professional courtesy to be notified when she was in the building (for example, if she needed to meet with one of her daughter's teachers). Then I could be sure to not go near that meeting location or to lock myself in my room. I did not feel safe around Crazy.

The principal refused to give me that professional courtesy of safety because he said it was against the law. What? I just wanted to keep myself safe. He refused to help. I e-mailed the girl's teachers, informed them of the situation, and asked them to give me a heads-up if Crazy had an appointment to meet with them. They were cool with it and understood. But the principal e-mailed them and said, "Do not inform Miss Kennedy, as [Crazy] has a legal right to be in her daughter's school."

Yes, she did. And I had a legal right to be safe at work. I was afraid of her. I said, "Just tell me, and I'll make myself invisible while she's in the building." He was adamant about how illegal this was. At this point, no one believed that I could be afraid of anything. It was because of my stupid mask.

I asked to have a meeting regarding this whole matter. I had never asked for help at this point in my life, so asking for this meeting was a big deal for me. A bunch of the top administrators, a teachers' representative, and I met.

One of them suggested, "Why don't we give Molly a professional, courtesy heads-up when [Crazy] is in the building?" I asked him to repeat that. I told him that had been my suggestion, but the principal had said it was illegal. The administrator countered that there was absolutely nothing illegal about it. It was a simple solution, and it made sense. The principal was squirming in his seat because he had gotten caught in his make-believe world of nonexistent laws. He also hadn't wanted to rock the boat and risk his tenure, which would allow him to keep his job until he retired. He was like a lot of people who are looking out only for themselves.

This is a long story to get to the point of why I gave away my power to this principal. I couldn't stand him from that point on. It didn't matter what he said or did afterward—my filter was focused only on how much I hated him because of the way he had handled this case. See, for most of my life, the people who were supposed to have my back didn't. I got kicked to the curb—physically, emotionally, and mentally—many times. For me, it was one more instance of someone who was supposed to support me treating me like garbage to protect his own interests and showing me that I'm not worthy. I was enraged.

It was so maddening. And let's remember, I had saved the school district from a huge lawsuit that would have been filed if I'd hit Crazy back. I had demonstrated excellent role-model behavior to my girls and had put their safety before mine. Other than the parents of the girls and some of my teacher friends, nobody really seemed to care. Crazy could have had a weapon, for goodness sake. What world was I living in? I was so disappointed and hurt. For me, those emotions showed up as anger, resentment, and bitterness. I should probably add rage. I felt like the hurt fifteen-year-old who hadn't dealt with her stuff. It always comes back to bite you.

I let people ruin my day(s) because I gave away my power. My principal didn't ruin my day; I allowed my disdain for him to ruin my day. I'm not excusing his behavior. Life has a tendency to put these kinds of people in your life. It's all about how you handle it. It was completely my choice. I missed out on a lot of happiness and productivity. My fault, my choice.

I'm still learning how not to let somebody's negative soundtrack become *my* soundtrack. I don't have to take everything so personally, and neither do you. Sometimes it's best to get out of your own way. You have enough obstacles in your life. Don't be one of them. As I said, I'm *still* learning this.

I was trying to look different on the outside compared with how I was feeling on the inside. I had constructed a mask that told everyone I was athletic, strong, and fit. That wasn't so bad at first. I was focused on achieving my academic and athletic goals—the harder the goal, the better. But it started to take on a life of its own, especially when I became a teacher. I thought that if people perceived me as tough on the outside, then they would think I must be tough on the inside. And that made it easy to keep people at bay by putting up my wall. That way, I didn't have to deal with my trust issues, and I could let people know me only a little bit. That mask kept my stuff secret.

Had people dared to look behind my mask, they would have seen a very fragile Molly. After the Crazy incident, my mask was starting to crack, and things were about to explode like a volcano. I could keep my bitterness, hurt, anger, and rage buried only for so long. Look out, I was about to blow up.

I love that I get to use my story to help teens rewrite theirs. For example, one time, after I presented my assembly to a high school, a senior boy stayed behind to talk to me after all the other students had left. He was very fit and strong. He seemed nervous, as if he had something to get off his chest. He finally told me that when he was younger, he'd been sexually assaulted (raped) by someone in his community. I share this because he ripped off his mask that day. By speaking his truth and not stuffing it deep down, he forever changed the course of his life. Instead of numbing himself with alcohol and drugs, he can talk about it to heal. Instead of taking out his anger on his girlfriend, he can deal with his anger in healthier ways. I am so proud of this boy. He had the courage to own his story and the chapters that others had already written for him. He now has the ability to become the author of his future. #flipyour20.

So which masks do you wear?

- "Oh, I'm fine. I don't need any help."
- "I can handle it myself."
- "I have great grades, so everything's perfect."
- "My [boyfriend or girlfriend] and I are super happy all the time."
- "I smile all the time, which proves all is well."
- "My clothes are expensive. Money equals happiness."
- "I am always in a relationship because I have so much love to give."
- "I'm an athletic all-star."
- "All the teachers love me."
- "I have anger issues."

It's exhausting wearing your mask, and you know it. Think about when you go home and you're all alone in your own head. Are you really OK? If not, let someone know. If not, why keep pretending and faking as if everything is OK when it's not? Nobody's life is perfect. Take off your mask.

Talking about it will help you change the way you view your circumstances. It's easier said than done. But we are such a head-down society, looking at our phones and devices, that we don't connect anymore. Let me clarify.

Sure, we are all connected via apps, the Internet, and so on. But we don't have face-to-face connections. Lift your head up from time to time. Make eye contact with somebody. When you take off your mask, people actually see you. I mean, they really *see* you.

Only you can control you. That's it. There are no other options. When you choose your filter, take control of your mind-set, and take off your mask, you take charge of your life. It feels great! I did it. Tag, you're it.

Your Turn

1. How can you relate to my story of feeling wronged by someone who you believed should have had your back or known better?

   _____

   _____

   _____

2. When was a time you felt disrespected (for a big or small reason) and held on to your anger/frustration for too long?

   _____

   _____

   _____

3. Did you try to come to a resolution? Why or why not?

   _____

   _____

   _____

4. If you're still carrying those feelings in your heart and mind, how are they holding you back? (Yes, they are.)

   _____

   _____

   _____

5. What are you missing out on because you are giving someone's actions or words meaning and power?

   _____

   _____

   _____

CHAPTER 4

Be Resilient

• • •

MY CIRCUMSTANCES SET ME UP to be a hot mess. I should probably be a high-school dropout, in jail, an addict, or dead.

What are your circumstances setting up for you?

I have good news. *You* decide; your circumstances do not. How you deal with your stuff is up to you. Keep moving forward. When you want to give up or feel overwhelmed, the tide often will turn in your favor. Sometimes your biggest success comes immediately after your biggest failure or disappointment. Push through the dip. Keep moving forward, forward, forward.

Webster's Dictionary defines *resilience* as follows:

* "the capability of a strained body to recover its size and shape after deformation caused especially by compressive stress"
* "an ability to recover from or adjust easily to misfortune or change"

Instead of being annoyed and making excuses when bad things happen, go against conventional wisdom. Marinate in the problems. Exfoliate with the frustration. It is in those moments that you truly have the opportunity to learn, grow, and develop the grit necessary to overcome challenges you will face again and again.

There isn't one successful person I know of or have read about who has found success the easy way. Feel free to interpret success however you want. I don't believe that the easy way is actually a thing. Whether successful people are athletes, celebrities, or business owners, they have all made a ton of mistakes and have been knocked down repeatedly. What has made them successful is that they got back up *every single time.* They also didn't reach success alone. They surrounded themselves with people who supported them, challenged them, and had a similar vision.

Every successful person has had a challenging path to reach his or her potential. Every. Single. One.

Here are a few real-life examples of how difficulties can help turn you into the person you deserve to be, if you choose. All these successful people had to be resilient to get where they are today. There are no shortcuts.

OPRAH WINFREY

Oprah—one of my favorite people of all time—has said, "Challenges are gifts that force us to search for a new center of gravity. Don't fight them. Just find a different way to stand."

Oprah is a woman of extremes: she is extremely successful, extremely powerful, and extremely passionate about what she does. But her success has come at the end of a long road of other extremes: obstacles. She grew up poor in the segregated South. She was sexually abused and had a child at fourteen, whom she lost. She started to get her act together when she was sent to live with her father.

Oprah faced both racial and gender discrimination in the world of American broadcasting in the 1980s and was even more determined to succeed. Despite the blows she was routinely dealt, Oprah never stopped fighting to achieve her goals. She became the youngest news anchor and the first black female news anchor at Nashville's WTVF-TV.

She reinvented herself as a talk-show host and used her ability to relate to people to propel her into becoming the most successful female television talk-show host of all time.

According to Oprah, "We are each responsible for our own life—no other person is or even can be." That's why it is crucial not to let challenges—whether they're events, people, your own characteristics, or other uncontrollable factors—act as barriers between you and your goals.

Oprah has said, "Energy is the essence of life. Every day you decide how you're going to use it by knowing what you want and what it takes to reach that goal, and by maintaining focus." Overcoming the obstacles present in your life is precisely what will give you the confidence to achieve your goals.

Oprah has also said, "You are built not to shrink down to less but to blossom into more. The right to choose your own path is a sacred privilege. Use it."

I love her.

Nelson Mandela

When Nelson Mandela was sent to jail for his opposition to apartheid in the 1960s, no end to the all-powerful apartheid system of South Africa was in sight. But against the odds, Mandela played a critical role in bringing about not only the end of apartheid but also the first truly democratic elections. He later became president.

ELLEN DEGENERES

Ellen, and the character she played in her sitcom, came out as gay in 1997. Her show was canceled the next season. Nobody in Hollywood was willing to hire her, because the sensitive and polarizing topic of homosexuality scared away advertisers. Years later she was back on TV hosting her successful talk show *The Ellen DeGeneres Show*. She was a pioneer in changing how people view homosexuality. She did it with grace and dignity. She ends each show with "Be kind to one another."

J. K. ROWLING

J. K. Rowling became the world's best-selling children's author despite managing on welfare benefits as a single mother. Initially, several publishers rejected her manuscript for *Harry Potter*. You know how her story ended up.

DWAYNE "THE ROCK" JOHNSON

In 1995, Dwayne had seven dollars in his pocket. The next year he was wrestling at flea markets for forty dollars a night. "The Rock" is now one of the biggest movies stars grossing over one billion dollars at the box office.

He has said, "Embrace the grind, lower your shoulder, and keep driving forward. Change will come."

KYLE MAYNARD

Kyle Maynard was born with no arms or legs. His love for sports started with playing youth football, and then he became a member of his highschool wrestling team, where he won thirty-six matches. He accomplished the feat of climbing Mount Kilimanjaro without the use of his prostheses.

TYLER PERRY

Tyler Perry may have a slew of movies in movie theaters every year, but it wasn't always that way. He suffered abuse as a child, both physical and sexual, and he never felt safe. To get through periods of abuse, he would think of his family.

"I could go to this park (in my mind) that my mother and my aunt had taken me to. I'm there in this park running and playing, and it was such a good day. So every time somebody was doing something to me that was horrible, that was awful, I could go to this park in my mind until it was over," Perry said.

EMINEM

Few others have spoken as openly about their troubled life as Eminem. Just read his biography or listen to his songs. He grew up in a trailer home, battled domestic violence as a youngster and in his own relationships, and was bullied among his peers. But Eminem rose above that and became a best-selling artist.

You are not alone when you are going through adversity.

* Bill Gates' first business failed, and he was fired by the company he founded.
* Jim Carrey used to be homeless.
* Bethany Hamilton had her arm bitten off by a shark and continues to surf.
* Stephen King's first novel was rejected thirty times.
* Thomas Edison failed one thousand times before creating the lightbulb.
* Jay-Z couldn't get signed to any record labels, so he created his own.

* Simon Cowell had a failed record company.
* Charlize Theron saw her mother kill her father.
* Steven Spielberg was rejected from the University of Southern California film school three times.

You can be resilient whether you deal with your stuff or not. It will take a lot longer if you don't. Sooner or later, your stuff will catch up with you. Count on it.

Remember the story about Crazy and my principal? I was an adult at the time. But in my mind, I felt as if I were a teen again in that moment, because to me the principal *represented* all the people who had failed to support me. Once again, I was being shown that I was a piece of garbage. I knew this story line all too well. I hadn't dealt with my stuff at that point. My stuff was crammed so deep down inside me that it finally took traumatic situations to start my unraveling process.

I mentioned my first significant event in chapter 3. This next event and how it was handled was the final straw in me coming undone.

EVENT TWO: GUN STORY

I had a student in my classroom with a gun. It was Friday, September 11, but not *the* 9/11. It was during the first full week of school. Here's what happened.

I ran a very tight classroom, and my expectations were ridiculously clear. I was a mix of a stand-up comedian and a drill sergeant. My reputation preceded me. The word in the halls was, "Follow Miss Kennedy's rules, be respectful, do your work, and it'll be a blast. Do the opposite, and it will be rough."

The incident occurred in a tenth-grade class. We had already reviewed 20 Cent and were learning about proactive and reactive behavior. Proactive behavior involves acting calm, cool, and collected during frustrating times. It's like a bottle of water: even when life shakes you up, you keep your cool. At the other end of the spectrum is reactive behavior. When life shakes you up, you explode like a bottle of soda. By the way, *The 7 Habits of Highly Effective Teens* by Sean Covey is a great book. We based part of our curriculum on it.

Most of the students had been in my class or knew me from freshman year. I had a couple of my basketball players in the class, too. I asked the students to close their eyes and put their heads down so that I could ask some personal questions and they could raise their hands honestly and without judgment. It's a good strategy to elicit honest answers.

After my questions, I told them to open their eyes and lift their heads. All but one student did. He was a new student. He wasn't a rude kid, but he was very squirrely and not used to consistency and boundaries.

I'd already spoken with him a few times that week, and I only saw my classes every other day. But I've always had a soft spot for kids like him, so our chats were stern yet nurturing.

"Miss K, I don't want to get on your bad side. I like you," he'd say.

"OK," I'd say. "Then I need your behavior to get on my page. Notice how the other students are behaving. Meet my expectations."

Back in the class, he finally lifted his head. But he seemed extra agitated and was still distracting kids around him. I instructed the other students to work independently, and then I went over and whispered to him that he needed to get focused, follow directions, and knock off the antics. I did this discreetly, and he was not embarrassed or put on blast.

Remember the proactive and reactive lesson plan?

He kept up his disruptive behavior, so I told him to stand out in the hall. He stayed at his desk. I stayed proactive and calm like water. I repeated myself more sternly each time. Finally, he got up, walked past me, and started to turn back toward his seat. I said, "Get in the hall." He said he wanted to grab his bag. I said, "Absolutely not. Get in the hall." I used this strategy because he would need to come back and get his bag after the bell rang, which would allow us to chat and work on resolving the issue.

After a few minutes, he knocked on the door. Then he knocked again. For the kids who knew me, their eyes were saying, "Dude, you better stop. You do not want to mess with her. Her bark is downright scary." Still, I stayed calm like water. This was very tough for me, because I hated having my class interrupted. I know *hate* is a strong word—that's why I'm using it. I half stepped into the hallway briefly; he was professing his need for his bag. I refused because if I relented, he would walk off with no resolution or closure. I said sternly, "You had better stop interrupting my class. When it is over, you may come get your bag. Do not interrupt my class again."

I returned to class. All was calm and peaceful. After all, if I'm teaching how to be proactive, I'd better darn well demonstrate it. I wanted to go off on him so badly. I kept telling myself to be a good role model, to model this behavior so that my students could see what it looked like in real time.

The door opened. Because my class ran like a well-oiled, efficient, focused machine, my students were in the zone. They were reading and unfazed. They kept taking turns reading aloud. I didn't look up, either. I figured it was a student coming in late who would quietly sit down and get on task. Nope. It was the disrupter.

I sensed him walking behind me. I was thinking, "You did *not* just walk back into my room after I kicked you out!" I turned my head to the left. "What do you think you're doing?" I asked him. At the same time, I reached out and grabbed his T-shirt sleeve.

He pushed my hand away. "I'm getting my bag," he snapped.

Pause. My students were now frightened for this boy. I could almost hear their thoughts. "You don't disobey Miss Kennedy. She's a control freak and super stubborn. Don't break her rules. She says what she means and means what she says. We will pray for you."

My thoughts were, "Oh, it's on. Over my dead body will you disrupt my class again and get your bag." Be careful what you wish for. I maneuvered myself so that I was between him and his bag. He started coming toward me. For a moment, I wondered if he was Crazy's son. I stuck my arm out to signal him to stop. He kept coming and walked right into my hand. Now my hand was pushing into his pectoral muscles. Fortunately, I was physically strong, headstrong, and a bit of my own kind of crazy. I repeatedly told him to stop and get out. After a few attempts to move forward, he saw that I was winning this one, and he finally left. I told him to go down to the dean's office.

My class and I continued our peaceful lesson on proactive versus reactive behavior. It was painful to remain as calm as I did. I think I shocked myself that I could do it.

Then my class was interrupted again. This time, it was the dean's assistant, who also happened to be that interim basketball coach who'd left those three girls unattended in the locker room. He never took ownership of his mistake with that situation, so I wasn't a huge fan of his. He told me that the disrupter wanted his bag; therefore, something must be in it. He asked if I could give it to him. I calmly walked over, grabbed the bag, and handed it over in the hallway. Meanwhile, my students were taking turns reading and answering questions. I loved those kids and their focus and discipline.

Two more periods were left in the day. Word started to spread that the cops had come and taken the kid away.

The principal (yes, the same principal I didn't like) called me at home around 4:30 p.m. to tell me that the kid had had a gun in his bag. A gun! The principal was calling to get my side of the story. Through my initial shock, I told him in *great detail* what had happened. Because of who I am and how I run my classroom (through structure, expectations, and follow-through), the kid had been caught, and nobody had been hurt or killed. It turned out he'd had the gun on him to protect him from people threatening him on his way home. The good news was that he hadn't planned on shooting up the school. The bad news was that he had brought a gun to school—and in my classroom!

Now all the what-ifs started to creep into my mind. Because I was stubborn and meant what I said and said what I meant (once I kick you out, you stay out, and you will not come get your bag whenever you want), what if I'd set him off? How easy would it have been for him to snap, especially because he'd known a gun was in his bag? Excuse me, Captain Obvious, but he didn't want to get caught, and he could have done everything in his power to get that bag back. What if I hadn't physically stopped him? What if he'd gotten it back and pulled the gun out? What if he'd shot my students? What if he'd shot my players in the class? What if he'd shot himself? What if he'd shot me? What if he'd shot someone on his way home? What if one of those guys had shot him? What would

I have done if he'd pulled it out in class? Would it have ended peacefully? Bloody?

Welcome to posttraumatic stress disorder (PTSD). I couldn't sleep for weeks. What if? What if? What if? Holy crap, I potentially saved someone's life. Holy crap, that could have turned out horrible.

Then the news caught wind that a student had brought a gun to school. The details were very vague. The superintendent said, "At no point was anybody in danger." What? Are you kidding me? A kid had brought a gun to school. It had been in my class. Everyone who'd crossed his path had been in danger. Where were the empathetic souls in this administration?

The following Monday, an emergency meeting was called for all staff before school. The principal *totally* watered down the story I had told him and started to take credit and give credit to the dean of students. Are you kidding me? Now, I'm not an attention seeker. I simply wanted him to be honest and tell the truth. I was still so shaken and didn't like attention, but I knew that my teacher friends who really knew what had happened would want to ask me questions about it.

I started to get very antsy and emotional. I wanted to crawl out of my skin. I was trying not to cry in that meeting. Remember, I'm tough Miss Kennedy and apparently don't have any emotions. Stupid mask. It took every ounce of strength to keep it together. I couldn't get out of that meeting soon enough. I ran down to my classroom and started bawling my eyes out. I had about ten minutes to pull myself together before my homeroom came in. Then I had to be fun, crazy Miss Kennedy. I wanted to curl up into a ball. But I couldn't tell anybody that. The show had to go on.

Someone had brought a gun into my classroom, and I was still trying to act as if I could handle it. What was my problem? Part of my mask was, "I don't need help, and I don't ask for help. Asking for help is weak."

Masks are stupid. This mask was cracking, and I was dying inside.

The next time my class met, nobody came in to debrief the kids. Nobody came—not the principal, not the superintendent, not the counseling department. None of the administration said thank you or asked how I was doing. Remember, when you hear something long enough, you start to believe it. I was hearing the same tune that I had growing up: "I'm not worthy or valuable. I'm a disposable piece of garbage." Again, what you don't deal with when you are young will absolutely come out later in life. In my mind, I was still fifteen (which was one of my worst years).

So I debriefed the class by myself. I tried to keep it together, wondering, "Why isn't an administrator or counselor helping me?" My counselor friend stopped by at the end of the day to check on me. She said she could tell that I'd been starting to lose it in the meeting and wanted to know if I needed anything. I said that it would have been nice if someone had debriefed the kids. I hadn't known what I was doing and hadn't even thought to ask, because I was still traumatized by the event. I had assumed that somebody would automatically show up to say something.

I was terrified to let people see me crack. However, being assaulted by Crazy, living through the gun incident, and then receiving limited compassion and empathy forced my hand. The volcano that was Molly was starting to smoke.

Another day or so passed. Not one administrator in the district checked in with me to say thank you or to ask how I was doing. Not one administrator asked if I needed anything. Again, this experience stemmed from my stuff about how people had failed to support me when I was growing up. The cracks in my mask were starting to show. Watch out!

I scheduled an appointment with the principal, assistant principal, and dean of students, because I had to ask why they hadn't checked on me.

Asking for this meeting was a big deal for two main reasons. First, I had decided to talk about it and get answers instead of stuffing my anger down like I always had up to that point. The second reason is that I wasn't sleeping. I couldn't. I kept asking what-ifs.

They didn't invite the assistant principal. They said she didn't even know what was going on, and there was no need for her to be there. Apparently, they didn't get along. It was clearly a dysfunctional administration. I don't think the dean showed up, either. I can't remember through my anger and rage in that moment.

I asked the principal why he had never checked on me. With the PTSD, sleep deprivation, all the what-ifs, and so on, I was trying to keep it together and not start sobbing. The gun incident had shaken me to my core. He said to me, "I didn't even think about checking on you because you're Miss Kennedy. You're so tough."

Pause.

In that moment, I imagined being Lindsey Lohan's character in *Mean Girls* when she flies across the lunch table and attacks the blond girl. Those words sent a jolt of rage through me that I didn't expect. Are you kidding me? The student had brought a gun.

"I'm not a superhero," I said. "I don't catch bullets with my teeth."

I continued asking if he would have checked on any of the other female teachers in the building if this had happened in their classrooms. He said yes. I asked whether he would have checked on any of the male teachers in the building if this happened in their classrooms. He said yes. What? So I was literally the only teacher he would not and did not check on.

He continued, "Just so you know, this hasn't been easy for me. I went home and hugged my family so tight because, just like that, it can be over. It has really made me question my mortality. This has been life altering."

What? He hadn't even been there. By the time the dean had retrieved the student's bag, and the principal had been called down, the kid had already admitted what was in there. The gun had been secured. The principal wasn't directly involved in the dangerous part of this incident. And it had all been because of me and how I run a classroom, because of my expectations, and because of my consistency and follow-through. Now, all of a sudden, the principal's life was altered? He wanted me to feel sorry for him? And he hadn't even checked on me. I was the most affected because I had physically stopped any potential injuries or deaths. But he was taking credit and giving the dean credit, and apparently I was a superhero who fought crime in my spare time.

I started looking around the room thinking I must be on a hidden camera show, because this was ridiculous. This could not be for real. Then the principal pulled out an excuse. "I get so busy with my to-do list, meetings, and data that I don't pay attention to the human aspect."

Oh my God! He ran a school with a thousand souls in it. I told him that he should start, because without the human aspect (i.e., human beings, and especially teens, for that matter), he didn't have a school. Isn't the human aspect the most important thing in a school?

That was my final straw. I was so angry, hurt, and bitter. I could no longer hide behind my mask. I was so enraged that I thought I would hurt myself or someone else. I envisioned punching out the glass in the principal's office door as I left. I didn't, but I really wanted to.

All my deep-down stuff was coming up and out, and I didn't have the strength to keep it down anymore. Twenty years was long enough. I returned to my classroom and started sobbing uncontrollably. The principal notified the counselors that I might need to talk about what had happened last Friday. Geez, you think? Two counselors came to my room. I was still sobbing. I told them I needed a recommendation of someone to talk to because of the way the gun incident and the Crazy incident had been handled and because they had brought some really old stuff to the surface. I was on the verge of snapping on me or someone else. It didn't feel safe to be in my own mind right now. I asked them to please give me some names of counselors.

Side note: A few years later, I came across a newspaper article where the dean provided information about how *he* had handled the gun incident, and he was applauded for how well he had responded and kept everybody safe. Some people have very selfish motives.

I'm writing about this story in the tone of how I felt at the time. I don't want to dilute my anger or thoughts for you. Let's keep it real, folks.

I like to go against conventional wisdom. As much as I still do not like that principal and how he treated me, I am thankful he was put into my life. Because of him being so selfish and insensitive, I was forced to have a much-needed meltdown and finally talk about my stuff. I couldn't keep my stuff buried any longer.

Later in that school year, budget cuts meant that some teachers were going to lose their jobs. This was the first round of teacher cuts, so everybody was on edge. That decision was up to the building principal. Guess whom he cut? Yep, yours truly. It was one more reason to hate him, as if I needed any more reasons.

I am thankful that his dislike of and discomfort around me made his decision easy. Fortunately for him, it required little explanation to get rid of me. I am now thankful for losing my job, because it forced me to follow my true dream, vision, and passion, which is traveling across the country and speaking to teens about the importance of resiliency and dealing with their stuff now rather than later.

Your Turn

1. What is one frustrating, disappointing, unfair, or hurtful situation you've experienced?

    _____

    _____

    _____

2. Did you deal with it and move on? How? Can you use that to help you when you encounter the next frustrating or unfair experience?

    _____

    _____

    _____

3. If you didn't deal with it, why not? How is it affecting you? (Yes, it is.)

    _____

    _____

    _____

4. Are you still harboring resentment? Is it because you are still wearing your mask?

    _____

    _____

    _____

5. What will it take for you to take off your mask and deal with it head-on? Whatever it is, do it.

    _____

    _____

    _____

CHAPTER 5
Chasing Evil

• • •

MY UNRAVELING WAS NOW FULL-BLOWN. As my mask was cracking and my layers were pulling back, I had an unsettling realization.

I was following the same career path of my molester. Essentially, I was becoming her—minus being a pedophile, of course. She was a well-respected teacher and coach. She was fun, and you didn't really want to get on her bad side. She was a coach who was tough and could get the most out of her team in practice and games.

I was virtually a carbon copy of those characteristics. I finally recognized it as I was spiraling out of control. It made me sick to my stomach, and I was coming unhinged, especially regarding the coaching part.

Basketball was my first love, and I was a jock and tomboy from as early as I could remember. Even when my mom wrote me off with that upkeep-and-maintenance letter, sports kept me sane and focused. I was lucky to have a superintendent, a principal, and an athletic director who allowed me to keep playing sports even though I didn't have health insurance anymore. I think they saved my life. I'm not sure if I'm being dramatic in saying that or if that was the reality of my situation at the time.

During that time, I tried to legally become an emancipated minor, but that never happened. I can't remember why.

It's important for you to know that I am much too competitive for my own good. I think competitiveness and wanting to win were my way of proving my value.

The intense mind-set I brought to coaching was a blessing and a curse. I loved coaching, and I hated coaching.

I loved it because I knew sports would help my girls in the future. Discipline, perseverance, resilience, teamwork, and communication are transferrable skills to every aspect of life. Girls who succeed in sports succeed in life. I wanted to help them succeed in a way that no one had ever shown me.

While my girls were running laps, I would often say, "Don't cut the corners. You cut corners now, you'll cut corners in life. Successful people don't cut corners. Do it right." There was a method to my madness and always a real-life lesson to be learned.

I never wanted to let my girls down. It was subconscious at first, but then it became obvious to me later on. (It took me a few minutes to write that last sentence because I started to cry. This is the shortest but most emotional chapter for me to write.) I would get so emotional about sports and doing right by my girls. The right thing was such a strong motivator for me. By being the best role model I knew how to be, I was trying to undo what my coach had done to me.

I did this with a strong moral compass and strict boundaries. I pushed my girls to their limits and got them to believe in themselves regardless of what others thought. And I taught them to never give up and to be confident in a way that most teenage girls aren't.

I was certainly not perfect. I can tell you that, and I'm certain my girls would tell you that. I was treating them in the way I wish I had been treated. I wanted them to have a better experience than what I'd had. They deserved the best I could give them. I had also deserved this as a teen but unfortunately had not been afforded the same respect.

Once I recognized the parallels, I knew I had to stop coaching to preserve my sanity. I barely slept during the basketball season. I would stay up thinking about what drill would solve the current problem we were having. I was always compelled to find a solution. My girls deserved it. If I asked them to give 100 percent, then I was obligated to do the same. If we didn't play well, I would feel as if I'd personally let them down, even hurt them. It ate away at my heart a little each time. It was killing me.

For a few years, off and on, I had mentioned I was going to resign from coaching. Nobody believed me because I was very committed and loyal. I was Coach K, and Coach K didn't quit.

The guilt and the thought of letting the girls down or looking like a quitter were powerful. So I sucked it up and continued to coach a few more years. It was mentally and emotionally excruciating.

I should note that I had *awesome* girls. I was one of the luckiest coaches around. My girls busted their butts; did everything I asked; and were cool, well-rounded people. I was also fortunate that most of their parents were amazing people, too. In my eight years of coaching, I had only one major problem with a parent. I received an anonymous ransom note of sorts in the mail because his or her child wasn't getting enough playing time. Seriously, that happened.

That incident had a severe effect on me. I couldn't believe that a parent was accusing me of being unfair or shady and hurting one of my girls. It was devastating, because I poured my heart and soul into doing the best I could for my girls. I was heartbroken.

I realize this may seem a bit dramatic, but remember, sports were my life-line from way back. Most of my stuff is intertwined with my experiences as an athlete. Athletics is in my mental and emotional DNA.

How could anybody think I would do anything to hurt my girls? I knew what it felt like to get hurt by my coach, and I would never hurt them. This is another example of how not dealing with your stuff will always come back to haunt you. This all was happening fifteen to twenty years after I'd been molested. Nobody else knew about my stuff and how deep the wounds were. My wounds were still so raw that I often overreacted when somebody struck a nerve. I was always in survival mode. It was exhausting.

I did eventually resign from coaching to keep my sanity and stop chasing evil. The irony is that I found out that the principal had cut my teaching job about a month later.

Your Turn

1. Are you are currently doing something, by choice or not, that is harmful or unsatisfying to you in some way? What is it?

   _____

   _____

   _____

2. How would you benefit if you walked away from doing that thing?

   _____

   _____

   _____

CHAPTER 6

Punch Fear in the Face

• • •

HERE'S THE THING ABOUT FEAR: it exists only in your mind. Sound familiar? It's part of your filter. You can't actually see fear. We interpret things and decide if we're afraid. There's nothing wrong with some of the fear we experience. Sometimes it can be lifesaving.

In fact, that's why we have the fight-or-flight response. A funny YouTube video shows a guy wearing a Halloween mask (an actual mask) and hiding in a big garbage bin next to a vending machine. When somebody walks by, the masked man jumps out and scares the person. Some people's fear response is to scream, run away, or fall to the ground. But one guy's response was different. He literally punched the masked man in the face. Fight or flight.

Sometimes fear shows up as your gut instinct. It's your internal check to keep you safe. It has a very high percentage of being right.

The fear that is important to discuss in this context is a different kind of fear—namely, the fear that is your 20 Cent and that is holding you back from reaching your optimal potential. It's all those lies you tell yourself so that you don't go after something you really want, such as asking that person out, trying out for the team, auditioning for first chair in orchestra, or applying for that internship.

Don't let your fear of what *could* happen make *nothing* happen. It's those times when you think, "I probably won't get it, so why even bother?"

You don't ever truly lose. You win or you learn. Yes, you might lose by not being selected to the team. But you learned what you need to improve on, or you learned that you weren't as into it as you thought, or you met some new people along the way. There is no shame in failing, only in never trying.

My biggest fears were having anybody find out about my stuff, asking for help, and looking weak. Pardon me, but I don't do weak. I used to think that asking for help or being vulnerable in any way was being fragile. I did everything in my power to hide and cover up all the bad stuff. It was exhausting.

I think—I know—I kept it hidden because I felt ashamed of what had happened to me and afraid of what people would think of me if they knew all my stuff, especially because of the tough I've-got-it-all-together mask I wore for so long. The toughest and bravest thing I ever did was ask my counselor friend to refer me to someone. It was time to go to counseling, because I needed to take off my mask. Actually, the right time had been twenty years ago. Better late than never.

Although I needed someone to talk to, and I knew it, I was still hesitant and resistant. I had spent the better part of twenty years covering up, building a protective wall with a moat and a fire-breathing dragon and flesh-eating piranhas around me, and it wasn't going to come down easy.

NEWS FLASH: that's why it would be awesome if you were stronger and more courageous than me and talked out your stuff *now*. It's never easy, but it's definitely going to get harder the older you get. The skeletons in your closet get nastier and nastier the longer they are locked up. Trust me on this one.

Six months after the gun incident, I finally called both counselors who had been recommended to me. I waited that long because I *still* thought I could probably handle it myself. I should have called right away, but I am too stubborn. Stupid mask. One of the counselors was covered by insurance but couldn't see me for a while. The second was not covered by insurance but could see me within a week. She was a little pricey for my blood, and I was fiscally responsible (OK, I was a frugal tightwad).

The latter counselor was the number-one option from my friend. I called the counselor and said that I'd like to make an appointment but that I really needed someone who wasn't going to put up with my crap. I needed someone who would tell it like it is and be brutally honest with me. If she was going to be sweet and delicate and all la-di-da, I wouldn't respond to that. She said that she was very honest and basically wouldn't throw unicorns and rainbows at me.

I made an appointment, but I wasn't really sure I believed she could handle me the way I needed so that I could break free of my pain. I was also pretty sure that I felt this way because I wasn't about to trust her very easily and was already coming up with reasons why it wouldn't work. "She probably won't understand, anyway." We are all very good at making excuses when we're afraid.

For my first appointment with her, I wore a specific T-shirt on purpose. It was a Nike shirt with an image of a cartoon heart with a face, arms, and legs. The heart was running, and the caption said, "I run to my own beat." I wore it so that she would be crystal clear that I was not somebody to be messed with. My shirt was me saying, "So, um, don't mess with me, lady. I'm always in control, so I'll run the show." More blah, blah, blah thoughts swirled around in my head to pump myself up and offset my fear of somebody knowing my deepest, darkest secrets.

We started talking. Within the first twenty minutes, I unloaded about all my stuff, even about being molested. What sort of magical powers did this counselor possess? She was only the second person I'd ever told at that point. I think I was sick and tired of being exhausted from carrying around all the emotional and mental weight of my stuff. It felt scary and awesome to get it off my chest and begin the process of healing and moving forward.

After I told her about being molested, she asked me if I'd ever molested anyone. I wanted to jump over the table, punch her in the face, and shout, "No! I've never molested anyone, you stupid jerk! I'm supposed to pay you for this session when you attack me like that? Woman, have you lost your mind? Do you know who you're talking to? How dare you! I come here and lay it all on the line, and you accuse me? Great. One more person to add to the list of 'you're supposed to have my back but don't.'" I was paying her to listen to me and help me, and she was being an idiot. Couldn't I catch a break?

Can you feel my anger and how I was always ready to push everyone away so that I didn't get hurt anymore? These reactions I had—and that you have—are defense mechanisms. We are trying to protect ourselves behind the mask *so much* that we get defensive over anything, big or small. Our ego and our hurt are doing that. My counselor had every right to ask me that question, because the cycle of abuse is very common.

We continued our first session, and I was swearing all over the place, finally getting some of my anger out. Then she stopped, leaned over the desk, and looked me dead in the eyes. With her hand waving in my direction and with a look of confusion and a stern tone in her voice, she said, "What's this? This tough-girl act. Is that real or just for show? What is this?"

In that moment, I wanted to slap her but simultaneously realized that she was a great match for me. You see, nobody had talked to me like that, ever. But she was calling me out on the carpet, just as I had asked and needed. I knew she would be the one to challenge me and force me to be honest with myself.

As I walked out of that first appointment, she said to me, "You won't be teaching forever. You'll be sharing your story with others."

She had no idea that becoming a youth speaker was my dream job at this point. But for her to have that intuition made me feel good about moving forward with her help. Magic powers indeed, woman.

As of this writing, I've had her as my counselor for over seven years. I was lucky to find a keeper on my first try. I speak with numerous teens who tell me they tried going to counseling but didn't click with the counselor, so they gave up on it. That's not OK. Sometimes it might take a few tries to find the right one. Or maybe it takes more than a few. But if you are on counselor number seventeen and there's still no fit, it may be time to look in the mirror. Take off your mask and let someone help you. There's no shame in your game.

One of the best decisions I ever made was going to counseling. I cannot emphasize this enough. It is the single most important thing I've done to release my anger, bitterness, and rage. It has allowed me to feel happiness, follow my true passion in life, and become the person I knew I was deep behind that mask. I encourage you to find someone, whether it be a trained professional or a trusted adult, whom you feel comfortable talking to. It will be life changing.

I used to think that being strong meant handling everything on my own. I was wrong. Being strong is doing what you need to do to find happiness and peace and living with integrity. Being strong and tough does not mean that you hurt people physically, verbally, or emotionally. Think back to Crazy. She wasn't tough because she physically assaulted me. I was tough because I did the right thing. *The right thing isn't always easy, but it is always right.*

Having courage means that you are willing to be vulnerable. (*Vulnerable* is a word that used to make me puke a little in my mouth. True story. More on that later.)

It's time to be brave and let people help you. Reach out to someone you trust, not your new friend who will probably not be your friend next month. Make a connection with a parent, relative, counselor, teacher, or administrator. Get your eyes off your phone, and look into the eyes of another person. Let that trusted person *see* you. You are worth being seen. You deserve to be seen, heard, and validated, because you matter. You really do.

Once I let people *see* me, took down my wall, and told my secrets and my stuff, I started to heal and finally began to get my life back. I remember being so afraid of letting people know my stuff and thinking that they wouldn't like me anymore or that they would treat me differently or not think I was as tough. The reality is, people were still my friends, and they ended up having more respect for me and were proud of me for seeking help. They all knew I needed help before I did. I think some of them were on the verge of having an intervention with me.

Facing your fears as I did can help in the long run in every aspect of your life. It definitely helped me find happiness and peace.

Facing my fears also helped me reach one of my bucket-list goals that I've had since I was little—that is, young. (I'm still little; I'm five feet one and three-quarters inches, to be exact.) I wanted to become an Ironman. Not the superhero guy but an Ironman triathlete.

I completed my first Ironman triathlon in Madison, Wisconsin (called Ironman Wisconsin, or IMWI). I'm not an endurance athlete. I'm naturally strong, quick, and powerful. I'm technically Ms. Kalamazoo 1998, a title I earned when I became a bodybuilding champion. That title will be the closest I ever come to Miss Congeniality. But if a movie is ever made about my life, I would like Sandra Bullock to play me. If any of you have a Hollywood connection, contact me!

I often show my bodybuilding pictures in my presentations, and students either say, "That's clearly a picture of a man," or vomit a little.

Anyway, for me, IMWI represents stepping out of my comfort zone and facing my fears. All Ironman triathlons begin at 7:00 a.m. and end at midnight. I had seventeen hours to do the following:

- Swim 2.4 miles in a lake (equivalent to swimming 10 times around a track).
- Bike 112 miles (equivalent to biking 448 times around a track).
- Run a full 26.2-mile marathon (equivalent to running 105 times around a track).

That equals 140.6 miles. Yes, I'm a little crazy—well, maybe a lot crazy.

This was way outside my comfort zone, because I almost drowned when I was eight. My nose plugs fell off, and the lifeguard had to come in and save me. When we got to the deck, I puked up a cherry cake doughnut. I still gag a little when I see one. Too much information?

I had been afraid of water from that point on. I let water scare me. It was my choice. My 20 Cent of water was so bad that even taking a shower and having water hit my face would cause me anxiety. Water owned me.

I gave my power away to water. But I knew I wanted to be an Ironman someday. I had to flip my 20 about water, and I had to start somewhere.

Day one of my Ironman journey began at my local pool, standing in the shallow end. The water was up to my chin. Don't laugh. We've established that I'm short.

My heart was pounding. I was sweating. I was freaking out. "What if I drown? No, I'll live." These thoughts went back and forth.

I'm an intense person, so major pump-up music played in my head: "We will, we will, rock you." All of this to reach my goal for the day of putting my entire head underwater and coming up alive. Are you jealous? No?

I made eye contact with the eighteen-year-old lifeguard and told him I was going to put my head underwater. If I started to drown, he could jump in and save me.

He looked down from his chair.

"Ma'am," he said. "If you start to drown, you can just stand up."

"Good advice. Thank you," I said.

Side note for the ladies: When somebody calls you *ma'am*, it means you look old. Unless you live in the South—then it's simply good manners.

I was still standing in the shallow end. My filter was flip-flopping between "What if I drown?" and "I'll live." Finally, I flipped my 20 and told myself, "I'll live. Just do it." I went under for about two seconds. Spoiler alert: I came up alive. I started singing in my head, "I am the champion of the world."

Then I took swim lessons. I'm not embarrassed to say that I used the water wings only once. I'm kidding. I used them twice. No, they were inner tubes, because my biceps are huge. Kidding again.

Look, life is about moving forward and making progress, not perfection. Perfection is not a human quality. You don't have to take a huge step. You just have to take *a* step. Keep moving toward your goals. I wanted to be an Ironman one day. I didn't have to be an Ironman on day one, but my day one was the first step to *becoming* an Ironman. You have to start somewhere. You have to believe it and want it for yourself through the highs and the lows.

Here is my challenge to you: What is your head-underwater moment going to be? What are you willing to do that scares you just enough, but doing it will help you achieve your goals and create the life you desire and deserve?

Take that first step *now.*

Nobody gets to hold you back from being the amazing person you are supposed to become. Stop holding yourself back. It's time to unleash your potential.

I could easily have chosen to let my fear of water hold me back and make that my excuse why I could never become an Ironman. I often meet people who tell me how cool it is that I did an Ironman triathlon. They quickly follow with how they would love to do one but then share a long list of excuses why they can't. One of the most common excuses I hear is that they aren't great swimmers, so that's why they'll never be an Ironman. Then I tell them about overcoming my fear of water, and they say, "Yeah, but I'm not a good swimmer." What? So you like water, you know how to swim, but you aren't Michael Phelps, and that's your excuse? So lame! Excuses are gross.

Please don't be one of those people. If you want to do something, do it! Maybe your head-underwater moment will be one of the following:

* Asking that person out
* Learning a new skill
* Trying out for that team, club, or school play
* Applying for that job
* Taking responsibility
* Being more of a leader
* Apologizing
* Forgiving
* Being a person of your word
* Starting to talk about your stuff

The struggle is part of the journey. I say, appreciate the challenges and the struggle. They are your opportunities to learn resilience, perseverance, and confidence. They get you ready for the next challenge, which always awaits.

Wishing things were different doesn't accomplish anything. You must take action. Change requires change.

Enough of the sad-face, slumped-over-shoulders excuses, such as:

* "I can't because I'm a victim of my circumstances."
* "I'll never figure it out."
* "All my teachers hate me."
* "I don't need your advice."
* "I know."
* "I'm not any good at that."
* "I'm not trying, because I tried it once and didn't understand."
* "I can't because _____."

Your Turn

1. What fears are holding you back from achieving something meaningful to you?

   _____

   _____

   _____

2. What fears/lies/excuses do you tell yourself to be "safe" from rejection or failure?

   _____

   _____

   _____

3. What prevents you from talking to someone and getting help with your stuff?

   _____

   _____

   _____

4. What is the *realistic* worst-case scenario if you start to deal with your stuff now?

   _____

   _____

   _____

5. What is the best-case scenario if you start to deal with your stuff now?

_____

_____

_____

6. What is your head-underwater moment going to be?

_____

_____

_____

CHAPTER 7

Marinate in It

• • •

DOOMSDAY WAS JUST AROUND THE corner for some teachers at my school. None of us knew who was going to lose his or her job because of budget cuts. I stood in the parking lot on doomsday eve with my nice guy colleague I mentioned in a previous chapter.

"I hope I lose my job tomorrow," I said to him. "I'm miserable. I'm not supposed to be here. I'm supposed to be doing something bigger. Give me five years, and I'll be traveling across the country speaking to teens."

I lost my job the next day. Be careful of the thoughts you put out into the universe. She's listening, and she'll follow through. Universe: 1, me: 0.

The moment I got home, with tears still streaming down my face, I immediately started searching youth motivational speakers on the Internet. Were there a lot of them? Were they mostly men or women? How could I become one? This was my opportunity.

I had known for many years that I was supposed to be using my story to help other people, especially young people. I envisioned traveling across the country speaking with students at schools, colleges, and teen leadership conferences. I had a message to share that I wish someone had shared with me when I was younger. It would have saved me twenty years of anger, resentment, and bitterness. When I first imagined sharing my story, I was still a few years away from even thinking about going to counseling, and there was no way I could have shared my story if I hadn't owned it yet. I knew I needed to come to terms with my stuff before I could share it from the stage.

I begin to immerse myself in the websites of youth speakers. I looked at their sites, their messages, and their calendars and consumed as much as information as possible.

Then I came across Josh Shipp. He's younger than me and has been speaking with teens since he was seventeen. He also began a coaching business for people who want to know how to become a professional speaker. His program is called Youth Speaker University (YSU), and it teaches people how to run their own speaking business. I opted in on his website and read as much free content as I could for the next two years. Basically, I cyberstalked him in the least creepy way possible.

During those two years, I was fortunate enough to have another school district hire me full-time. I was now a few years into counseling and really happy at my new job. It was such a good experience for me because I knew I could reinvent myself and didn't have to be my previous caricature of tough Miss Kennedy who catches bullets in her teeth and isn't afraid of anything or anyone.

At my new job, I taught kindergarten through fifth grade for the first semester and middle school for the second semester. I was used to teaching high school and coaching middle-school kids, and I didn't have much experience with the little ones. One of my girls was very concerned about me teaching little kids. "You know you can't talk to them like you talk to us," she said. "They are going to be terrified of you. Maybe you shouldn't take it." Sadly, I understood what she meant.

I was halfway through my first kindergarten class. (Those kids can be a tough crowd, because they get bored and distracted very easily.) Out of nowhere, a boy yelled out, "You crack me up, lady!" That was all the affirmation I needed to know I was in the right place. The little ones weren't afraid of me. I was able to act goofy, be animated, and entertain my classes in a fresh, new way. It was awesome.

Remember, what you see is what you get. I chose to see my new, younger audience as an opportunity instead of an obstacle. It was a fantastic two years.

Then I got cut from that job. It was less devastating the second time around. I like to say that losing my job twice was the best thing that happened to me. In my gut, I knew after two or three years of teaching that I had a bigger calling. For years, I had envisioned owning my own business, working my tail off, having freedom, and making a bigger impact on the lives of teens. My classroom could be a stage anywhere in the country. I wanted to share my story so that teens could rewrite theirs.

I was now beginning my third career. First, I'd been a certified athletic trainer (ATC). Then, I'd been a teacher. Finally, I was going to become a youth motivational speaker. So much for a straight career path.

Losing my job twice made me appreciate two of my favorite sayings even more. I often say, "Marinate in it" or "Don't poo-poo it." Basically, I'm saying appreciate the tough times, the unfair circumstances, and the things that make you want to have a pity party for yourself. It is in those times specifically that you truly grow, learn, develop, and transform into the amazing person you are supposed to become. A lesson is always there if you choose to see it.

Four years after that parking-lot conversation and losing my job the first time, I was flying across the country to California to speak at my first national conference for teens, and it came from Josh Shipp's recommendation. How cool is that?

I had imagined many times what it would be like to take that first flight required to reach my speaking destination. It was time. I prepared like crazy. I found my seat on the plane. "Oh my God! This is actually happening."

The key point is that it wasn't an accident that it happened. I'd worked my tail off implementing and taking action on everything I learned through YSU. I believe Josh noticed that, which was why he personally recommended me for this event. Fortunately, they were looking for a female speaker who had a story of resilience. That's me—the bounce-back girl!

It was time to go on stage. The room was filled with fifteen hundred teens and advisers from across the country and from military bases around the world. I was projected onto two huge screens so that the people in the back could see me. The energy in the room was amazing. I nailed it! The way the teens and advisers reacted afterward made me realize that my message was genuine, authentic, and impactful. I was living my purpose. It was bliss.

Had I not lost my job, I would not be living my dream. I'm not great at listening to life's whispers. But getting hit by a Mack truck as I did by losing my job is the appropriate volume for me to take note and take action.

I share this story to encourage you take a look at your life. When bad or unfair things happen, do you sit and complain about them? A pity party is fine, but make it brief and then move on. Or do you wallow in the injustice to the point where it holds you back for a long time or forever? Sometimes we need a swift kick of reality to move us in the direction of our goals.

Five years to the day of losing my job the first time, I texted that same nice guy colleague. We reminisced about that "give me five years, and I'll be traveling across the country speaking to teens" conversation. At that same moment, I was packing my bags and flying back to California for another speaking engagement.

Five years. Goals take time. If it matters to you, it matters. And you keep at it until it is achieved.

Create a vision. Take action.

To keep moving forward in creating a successful business, I had to make a lot of sacrifices. I spent less time with my friends. I wasn't able to go out for entertainment or buy things, because I needed to save money to invest in my business. I put in many hours on my own and isolated myself to get my business off the ground and maintain its success. It was difficult. But it was not impossible.

I must add that I was able to pursue this new career because my grandpa was willing and able to help me get it off the ground financially. I'm so fortunate to have him. Throughout this crazy life of mine, he has been my one constant.

Here is one of my favorite quotes, by Albert E. Gray: "The successful person has the habit of doing the things failures don't like to do. They don't like doing them either necessarily. But their disliking is subordinated to the strength of their purpose."

What are you willing to sacrifice (temporarily) to achieve your short- and long-term goals? If you answered, "Nothing," you aren't ready for change. If you answered, "Whatever it takes," you have the right mind-set and need to start taking action—today!

Some people ask me, "Can you even believe you are doing this? Is this beyond your wildest dreams?"

I reply, "I can believe it. This is exactly what I envisioned. I *am* living my wildest dream. The big, scary unknown for me was the timeline. I don't like the unknown. But I knew it would happen, because I knew I would work hard for it."

I don't say that to sound cocky. Trust me; there were plenty of times when I felt desperate in the beginning, hoping that somebody—anybody—would hire me to speak to their students.

You have to believe it, visualize it, and work your tail off to reach your goals. It's always worth it. If it matters to you, it matters.

Your Turn

1. What are some challenges in your life where, if you chose to flip your 20, you would see the opportunity (not the obstacle) staring you in the face?

    _____

    _____

    _____

2. Can you think of an example when something bad/unfair happened in your life and you were initially upset but turned it into a positive experience? Explain it here.

    _____

    _____

    _____

3. One of my *short-term* goals is: _____

    _____

    Two steps I need to take to make it happen are: _____

    _____

    _____

    I am willing to sacrifice _____ to achieve this goal.

4. One of my *long-term* goals is: _____

_____

Two steps I need to take to make it happen are: _____

_____

_____

_____

I am willing to sacrifice _____ to
achieve this goal.

CHAPTER 8
Circle the Wagons

• • •

I CANNOT SHARE MY EXPERT opinion of how my support system helped me when I was a teen, mainly because I didn't have one. But over the decades, I have learned the positive impact that support people can have if you are lucky enough to have them in your life.

It's important—dare I say, critical—to *always* have someone to talk to about anything at any time. I didn't have that in terms of family when I was growing up.

What I remember about growing up was becoming a very good liar by age eight or nine. In my house, we had to pick whose "team" we were going to be on: my mom's team or my grandparents' team. They didn't get along at all. My mom is the only child of my grandparents. I don't have any aunts, uncles, or cousins.

Picking my grandparents' team meant that I would go to church every week and report back to my grandma. She would always ask which priest had said Mass and what the sermon was about. To do this, I had to endure verbal harassment from my siblings about being a goody-goody and a spoiled brat of my grandparents. I would lie and tell them that I hadn't gone to church; I'd gone for a walk. They would tease me regularly about going to church, even though we were all raised Catholic.

Eventually, this became too much to handle at such a young age. To survive, I stopped going to church. When my grandma quizzed me, I would have to tell her lies about the priest and sermon. Becoming a good liar at that age was my initiation into becoming a survivor. I would need all my survival skills too many times to count.

At one point, my mom decided she wouldn't allow us to see our grandparents. I think it was her way of getting back at them. There were a number of times when my siblings and I would ride our bikes to the church to meet my grandpa. He would put our bikes in the trunk and drive us to my grandparents' house. We'd have lunch and he would drive us back to the church. We rode our bikes from the church to our house and lied by saying we were out for a bike ride.

When I got into middle school, my mom told me directly, "You don't talk about what happens inside this house to anybody else. What happens here stays here. We handle it in-house."

I would try to get my feelings out, but it was usually when I was so angry that I was about to blow. Then my mom would tell me, "Give me a break, Molly. You don't feel like that. Stop being so dramatic. Don't be ridiculous."

The tension in my house, which I called the 'structure' was palpable. I remember hearing my oldest sister talking about a major surgery my mom was having the following day. I asked her what she was talking about and why nobody told me. She said, "Well, Molly, you don't talk to anybody here, so we're not going to talk to you." I was thirteen, she was twenty.

Sadly, the only support I received at that time was from the person I trusted most, the same one who would later molest me. I thought she was being so kind and understood me and my feelings. What I now know is that she was doing something that all child molesters do. It's called grooming, or gaining the trust of the child little by little to see what the molester can get away with before he or she makes a move.

I share this in this chapter about support systems because I know how terrible it is to lack one. I also know that these experiences made me not trust anyone and prevented me from letting people support me and have my back. It's a long, hard road on your own. Let people be there for you. Life will be easier, and you will feel safer.

I was fortunate to have a few good friends from college, graduate school, and beyond. I would never claim to have a ton of friends. I have just enough for me.

The problem was that I never or rarely used them. Through my actions, I taught them that I didn't need help, advice, or whatever, because I could, would, and did figure it out on my own. My lack-of-trust wounds were deep.

I would often listen or be there to help them, mainly because that deflected the focus off me. The less we talked about me and what lay behind my mask, the better and the safer I felt at that time. Safe is good. I like safe—a lot.

As I started dealing with my stuff through counseling, I tried to open up to my friends little by little. I had a few friends who totally got it and were happy for and proud of me. That felt *so* awesome.

Some friends didn't recognize the changes or improvements I was making. This was disappointing because I would get comments such as, "Whoa, you never used to act like *this* before" or "That doesn't even sound like something *you* would say." They always said it in a tone indicating that they weren't comfortable with the "new" Molly. This made me feel as if I couldn't open up to these friends as I finally wanted to. At first I kept them at bay, but when I needed to bring them closer, sometimes it worked, and sometimes it was a disaster.

I chose to let go of some friendships that were one-sided or not supportive. It wasn't easy to do, but I finally realized that I only wanted people in my life who actively supported and encouraged me, and I did the same in return.

I also created brand-new friendships. I felt like I could truly be myself with them, because they didn't know the old, angry, walls-up Molly. I am grateful for these friendships.

I encourage you to make solid connections with good people now. Don't waste decades like I did. Most of these changes didn't happen until my midthirties.

I'd like to share another story that really challenged me to see if I was ready to use my support system. Or would I fall back into the same old pattern of "I can do it myself"?

I recently had an unfortunate/fortunate experience. That wasn't a mistake by the editor—I meant to say that. This experience was absolutely terrible. It was also remarkably helpful.

I competed in the Tough Mudder, which is a ten- to twelve-mile run with a bunch of obstacles and lots and lots of mud. Ergo, Tough *Mudder*. I teamed up with a high-school friend in January, and the race was in early August.

The weather was perfect. We had just completed the second-to-last obstacle, which involved running up a wall shaped like a skateboard ramp in the X Games.

We were happy and had one final obstacle left. I turned to my friend and said, "You know, considering all the crazy things we had to do today, it's pretty impressive that we have only a few bruises and scratches."

I should've known by then not to put comments like that into the universe; she has a sick sense of humor.

I was most looking forward to the last obstacle. It stood between us and the finish line about twenty yards away, and it was called Electroshock Therapy. You run from one end to the other, trying to avoid the long, yellow tendrils hanging down that have live electrical voltage running through them.

You're probably thinking, "Molly, why were you most looking forward to this obstacle?" If so, you're smarter than me.

Yes, I was looking forward to it because I was looking forward to being electrocuted. I know it sounds strange, but I promised you I would be honest.

My friend was least excited about this obstacle and hesitated for a bit. I was also nervous but excited. And I really just wanted to be done and have a restful evening at the campsite making s'mores.

I decided to just go. Maybe five steps in, I got zapped, and I dropped into the mud like a sack of potatoes. To say it was shocking would be lame. It was so startling. I felt like I'd been sucker punched by Rocky.

I was facedown in the mud, trying to catch my breath. Then I got up as if I were Rambo (Google him) and started charging forward. I took maybe two steps before getting popped again.

At this point, most normal people would have army crawled in the mud under the tendrils to the end. I tried to be normal once; it was the worst two minutes of my life.

What did I do? I'll give you one guess. Yep. I stood up again. Oh my God, what was wrong with me?

I covered some distance this time, and then POP! I was down again. I was so startled that I was sort of disoriented. How could this awesome obstacle defeat me so easily? I wanted to be tougher than it. I'm a little embarrassed to type that last sentence.

Still facedown and not wanting to get back up (finally), I heard the volunteers and spectators screaming, "Just crawl!" I army crawled the last few feet and cleared the voltage.

A volunteer handed me my well-earned orange headband and said, "Wow! That was one of the most amazing efforts I have seen today." Translation: "Woman, you are crazy. What is your problem?"

I crossed the finish line and bent over to catch my breath. I looked down and thought, "Uh-oh, I'm going to need a medic."

At some point during my three falls, I'd sliced my right shin open almost to the bone. Sorry if that grosses you out. It gets worse. Trust me.

There was an amazing medical tent on site. I got the wound cleaned out and was stitched up from the inside out. It was the first time I'd had stitches.

That was on a Saturday. Fast-forward two to three days, and my leg was in severe pain. It was starting to swell, and I was quite nervous. I got antibiotics, but the next day it started to leak near the stitches. And it smelled so nasty, as if raw sewage were dripping out of my leg. I clearly had an infection. I was freaking out.

The infection required two types of antibiotics. It also incapacitated me for two full weeks. I was literally laid up on the couch—no shower, no driving, no standing, no nothing—for two full weeks!

The excruciating pain came any time my leg was lower than my heart. The blood flow to the infection site was the worst pain I have ever personally experienced.

At times, I let out bloodcurdling yells. I couldn't help it. I was lucky that my neighbors didn't call 911, thinking that I was being attacked by an intruder.

The middle seven days were the worst. I had no strength left. I was sleep-deprived, which is a separate torture of its own. I had no appetite and lost about five to seven pounds lying there. I was most nervous about losing any muscle in my legs. (They don't call me Quadzilla for nothing.) OK, so I'm a little vain. Actually, I was most nervous about losing my leg. Had I waited too long to get treatment? Was it going to have to be amputated below my knee? My mind was spiraling out of control.

During that middle week, the only way I could get around the first floor of my house was to scoot around on my gluteus maximus. I had crutches and two kinds of walkers, but the booty worked best because my leg was flat, dragging on the ground.

My lower leg looked nasty. I was draining it all the time, and some disgusting chunks were coming out of it. Sometimes it looked as if a caramel macchiato were leaking out. Then it was draining blood. It was interesting to wake up on those mornings to look at the overnight carnage. Had someone broken into my house to rob me but instead decided to repeatedly stab my shin to death? It was a bloodbath.

OK, I had to share those details to get to why I consider this a fortunate experience. Thanks for playing along.

It was a blessing because it forced me to do something I am terrible at doing—that is, asking for and receiving help. I am notoriously bad at this.

I had posted on Facebook (that thing old people use) that I was laid up with an infection. Friends, former students, and people I hadn't seen in a long time came out of the woodwork to help. At first, I thought I'd be fine after only a day or two, so I didn't accept help then.

But as the days and then weeks passed, I couldn't do it by myself. I actively reached out for help. This may not seem like much to you, but for me this was groundbreaking. I still wasn't good at asking for help, and I'd been plenty uncomfortable receiving it.

My grandpa drove me to appointments. I needed friends to do my laundry, run a few errands, put stuff on the bottom shelf of the refrigerator because I couldn't stand to reach the top shelf, fill my water bottles, bring in the mail, empty my garbage can, close my windows and doors for the night, and mow my lawn, just to name a few tasks.

After two weeks, I finally got all of the infection cleaned out of my wound. I was left with a hole in my leg! It was gross. It was so deep we could have done chips and salsa out of that thing. It finally closed up and I have an impressive battle scar.

Are you wondering why I'm thankful for such a painful, debilitating, and nasty experience?

Here's why. A month earlier, I had told my counselor that I needed to get better at receiving help and kindness from others. I'd had a recent meltdown over this, and I wanted to get better. I asked her if she could give me some tips or homework to fast-track this whole "being OK with receiving goodness from others" thing.

She looked at me, confused. "You know that's not how it works. With everything you've improved on in the past six years, you can't manipulate situations to fast-track them."

I reverted to being thirteen and whined. "Just come on. You know I'll do what you tell me. Just tell me. Come on!"

She repeated, "I can't, and you know this."

I whined some more. "Ugh. I *know*! Just come on and tell me. Come on; just tell me what to do to fix this."

After a few more similar exchanges, I said, "Whatever. I'll figure it out on my own." I can be a brat sometimes.

Fast-forward a month, and we're back to the universe's sick sense of humor. Here I was, laid up with a wicked infection from an event I'd really wanted to do. At one point, I had to chuckle to myself. "Well, here's the fast track I was asking for." Universe: 2, me: 0.

Just like you, I still have quite a few improvements to make. Sure, I have a few more years under my belt. But when I look back at the tough times, I'm so grateful for them. I've learned to become resilient, to persevere, to never give up, and finally to ask for help. I now know that I will appreciate any challenge life throws at me. I will also be confident that I'll overcome that challenge. I've been through the wringer of life. Nothing can stop me now. I don't believe that this would have been the case if I'd had a more "normal" upbringing.

Again, don't poo-poo the hard times, but appreciate and marinate in them. They are excellent teachers.

Your Turn

1. Identify the people in your life you can go to no matter what. You may have different people for different topics. That's OK and normal. For example, maybe you go to your mom for questions about school problems, but you go to your dad for questions about relationships. Find what works for you.

   Whom do you talk to about your stuff?

   I go to _____ to talk about _____.
   I go to _____ to talk about _____.
   I go to _____ to talk about _____.
   I go to _____ to talk about _____.

CHAPTER 9

Forgiveness

• • •

Not forgiving is like drinking poison and
expecting the other person to die.

—BUDDHA

I AM AWESOME AT HOLDING grudges. World class, even. I think it's in my
DNA. I've been hypothetically drinking that poison for decades. I think
my heart and soul have died a little bit with each sip.

I'm very new at this forgiveness thing, but I will share my limited experience with you. I hope something will click with you and inspire you to
forgive someone in your life.

The first time I really, truly forgave someone for serious things wasn't until
I turned forty. In the decades leading up to this watershed moment, I had
so much anger, resentment, bitterness, hatred, stress, and tension built up
inside me. I'm sure I blamed certain people in my life for making me feel
all those yucky feelings. I'm also confident that I used those feelings for
survival and to prove to myself that I was better than my circumstances
and to prove my worthiness. As Brené Brown states in the audiobook, *The
Power of Vulnerability*, "it's easier to do than to feel." The more I *did*, the
more I achieved, the less I had to consciously feel. I achieved some cool

goals trying to prove that I was valuable. I now think that I did those things to chase my worthiness.

Despite all my stuff, I graduated fourth in my class, earned my master's degree by twenty-three, was a bodybuilding champion and gold medalist in the Empire State Games (New York) in Olympic-style weightlifting, and finished multiple marathons and triathlons, including the full Ironman triathlon of 140.6 miles. I was a homeowner and a well-respected teacher and coach.

I had come from being a fifteen-year-old runaway with a backpack filled with a couple of changes of clothes to being successful on many fronts. However, none of it made me feel complete or truly at peace and happy about how far I had come.

The thing that changed how I felt about it all was finally being able to forgive.

I started with my mom.

It was a bitter day in the middle of one of the coldest winters on record in my area. I'd just finished snowshoeing and stopped by the cemetery mausoleum where her ashes were located. She had been dead for seven years.

Before I go any further, it's important to note that death totally freaks me out. I sometimes wake up in the middle of the night in a miniature panic attack, thinking about death. I can't attend wakes or funerals because I'm a sobbing mess and not supportive at all.

The only time that was different was at my mom's wake. Long story short, I accidentally found out from a nun who used to work for my grandpa that my mom had died. Although I don't speak to my dad or the four middle siblings, perhaps one of them could have contacted my oldest brother or me to tell us. But that's how my family operates. It seems odd to those I tell but normal to me.

My brother took my grandpa earlier in the day so that he could say good-bye to his daughter. My siblings completely ignored them. To be fair, my grandma was a tough cookie, but my grandpa was a really good guy. He never hurt any of them.

I had a couple of friends drive me to the funeral home. I asked my brother for the layout of the place ahead of time, because I was going to be in and out quickly.

I put one of my friends in charge of finding out how my mom had died so that I could know my family history. I told my friends that if they turned around and I was gone, it was because I was already outside. They didn't think I was serious. I was in and out of the funeral home in less than five minutes.

As I made my way to the casket, I happened to pass my dad, my brother, and one of my sisters. I'm not sure if they saw me, but I had tunnel vision. I was on a mission and used my athletic focus to get in the zone.

At the casket, my heart was racing. It had been a number of years since I last saw my mom. I said the few things I needed to say to her—no tears— and left. Contrast this to when I was teaching and the elderly copy lady passed away, and I was sobbing uncontrollably at her casket. My mom's wake was my only experience with death where I didn't shed a tear.

Anyway, back to my mom's ashes at the mausoleum. The other times I'd been there, I'd wanted to punch out the glass and dump her ashes every-where. This time had to be different. I had to forgive her—for me. I had no idea where to start. I had never done this before. I could feel the old anger creeping in. I texted a friend to ask for some tips. I was resolute in standing there until I could do this. I needed this. I thought of it as another goal. I had to achieve this.

Just around the corner, a funeral service was beginning. This meant the traditional, sad violin music was playing. I started sobbing for that random person. The tears wouldn't stop. It was a blessing in disguise, because it was propelling me to have emotions other than anger and to give my mom forgiveness.

I went back and forth with anger and sadness, asking why over and over. Why did she have to be a drunk? Why didn't she come to get me after I left home? Why did she basically deliver me into the hands of a predator? Why?

It was hard to know that I was never going to get any answers. The closure would have to come from my side of things, from inside my heart.

And then it hit me like a ton of bricks. I had been giving her my power all these years later, even while she was dead. I had clung to my anger almost as a badge of honor to prove that I could be successful, despite her writing me off less than two months after I'd run away. With almost every goal I achieved, it was a slap in her face that I was strong enough to make it and didn't need her anyway. Sadly, I hadn't consciously recognized until all these years later that I was giving away my power to her. I was allowing her to still control me from her urn of ashes.

I didn't want to walk out until I felt in my heart, mind, and gut that I'd done it, that it was going to be time to let go. I didn't want to come back to this place physically, mentally, or emotionally.

It had been a solid forty-five minutes. There were a lot of tears. Did I do it? Did I do it right? I didn't have the handbook of rules of forgiveness, but I thought I'd forgiven her. When I walked out of there, a huge weight lifted from my heart. I had been carrying around such emotional baggage my whole life. For the first time, I began to sense something other than pent-up resentment. I thought that this is what happy must feel like. So far, I liked it.

My second forgiveness attempt came a few weeks later. This one was an even bigger deal than forgiving my mom.

I was speaking at an out-of-state event, which happened to be a few towns over from where my molester lived. I searched for her on the Internet and found where she worked. I contacted her earlier in the week via e-mail to meet me about a mile from her work. She didn't reply. I probably seemed like the Ghost of Christmas Past.

The day finally arrived. I was getting worked up and emotional. What if she actually showed up? Would I snap and beat her face in and go to jail? I like to think I'm tough, but I watch *Orange is the New Black* and am confident that I'm not prison tough. But I sure was enjoying the images of bashing in her face.

Would she deny what she did to me? Would she act as if it were no big deal? This could totally blow up in my face. I was nervous that all the hard work I'd put in during counseling could come undone and I would spiral backward. I was starting to think that it was a mistake to try to meet up. The meeting time was fast approaching.

Of course, like the pathetic coward she is, she never showed up.

I sat in the rental car and started to get angry. I thought back to everything she had done to me: the grooming, the manipulation, crossing every conceivable boundary (physically, mentally, emotionally), isolating me from others, molesting me while her husband and children were in the house, giving me alcohol, crossing state lines with me. The list goes on.

I reflected on how profoundly this had altered my heart, mind, soul, and life and how her choices to destroy me had been so selfish, sick, and successful in the most personal of ways. I was getting livid.

I had to stop myself and flip my 20. I wasn't there to get mad. I realized that this was the closest I would ever be to her again. I needed to do this— for me.

Sitting there, I finally had a few aha moments that struck me like lightning bolts. Knowing what I now know about sexual abuse and pedophiles, I'd been the *perfect* target. I'd been a kid who was lost and weak and had little to zero support.

I hadn't done anything wrong. She'd abused her power to abuse me. My conscience was clear. I was the innocent victim. She was the sick one who had to live with her decisions. Holy crap! What a terrible burden to live with. Deep down, I choose to believe she is tormented and guilt ridden by her decisions. I have thrived despite her. I can't believe I gave her my power for so long. So many wasted years. After years of not seeing her, I was still allowing her to own my mind. No more. The time is now!

I finally forgave her. It is something I never thought I would do.

At that moment in the rental car in the parking lot of a strip mall, not only did I feel happy, but I also was experiencing a new feeling: peace. I liked this one.

The third person on my list was my grandma. This would be three times within five months. I was on a roll.

When I was young, my grandparents lived one block over and kind of half raised me. When I look back at pictures, I was always dressed in sneakers and sporty outfits. I was a tomboy from the beginning. Give me sports, not dolls. I would play football and hockey with my brothers and their friends. They even put me in goalie pads when I was little. I loved it. My grandma didn't. She would scold my brothers for putting me in those dangerous situations.

"Molly is the baby. She doesn't belong here," she would say.

"But I'm having fun," I'd say.

As I entered middle school, she liked my sporty style even less. Keep in mind that my grandma was always dressed up beyond prim and proper. She was born in 1919 and came from a generation where "dressing like a lady" was the only option. She had lovely outfits, shoes, and jewelry, and God forbid she ever left the house without her pink lipstick.

When I would visit her and my grandpa during those oh-so-lovely and not-awkward-at-all middle-school years (yeah, right), she got her way. I'd walk in the door, and she would give me a disapproving look. She'd ask how much I weighed and then put me on the scale. The number was never low enough for her. She always asked, "Why do you weigh so much?" I didn't weigh a lot. I was always physically fit but never a twig. It was always too much for her. She would repeat the same story of how little she had weighed (114.5 pounds) her whole life. She also made it very clear that she maintained that weight without all this exercise nonsense that I did. She didn't understand through the years why I liked being strong and having muscles. At one point when I was in college or graduate school, she was so frustrated that she looked at me and said, "You look ridiculous with those muscles. Your arms look like a man."

I was devastated. I take such pride in my physicality, for how it looks, because it doesn't look like society's standard of beauty, and for the athletic accomplishments it has allowed me to achieve. Her comment was a punch in my gut.

After the middle-school weight shaming, she told me to go upstairs and change into the *nice* clothes she'd bought for me. Nice meant girly. As I write this, I can feel myself shrinking in shame. There's nothing wrong with new clothes, but these clothes were all about changing who I was. Then she'd clip a pair of earrings on me, followed by pink lipstick. I *hated* those moments. I've never cared for pink, but that was "old lady's" pink lipstick. Oh my God, it was so humiliating and shameful.

My grandma would take me out in public only when I was dressed in the girly clothes. Apparently, I was then "good enough" to be seen with her. I felt so worthless. I always wondered why I wasn't good enough for her. I wasn't into drugs or criminal activity. I had good grades. I was a good athlete. I was a person of good character despite having a typical adolescent chip on my shoulder. I wanted to be loved for who I was, for the content of my character. What did I have to do to make her proud? Would I ever be enough? Now I know that I was simply the unfortunate target of her perception of how young girls should dress.

I've never bought into the notion of putting out an image that isn't true to my character. I rebelled by not wearing makeup (I still don't), by not caring much about my hairstyle (or lack thereof), and by wearing only what makes me comfortable in my skin (usually that's sneakers, shorts, a T-shirt, and a hoodie). I'm confident that when I die, people won't say, "I'm not going to Molly's wake because, you know, she never really got dressed up; she didn't wear makeup; and she bucked most of society's stereotypical, gender-biased social and beauty norms." Seriously, those things just don't matter to me.

Going through all of this has definitely made me keenly aware of the importance of accepting people for who they are. Regardless of race, religion, sexual orientation, or expectations of others, people shouldn't be ashamed of being comfortable in their own skin.

Oh, right, back to forgiving my grandma. I was sitting in the mausoleum, looking up at her plot. I started replaying all the negative memories I referenced in the previous paragraphs. I was starting to get the hang of this forgiveness thing. I didn't get too angry this time. But I did feel very sad, and I was sitting there alone, sobbing uncontrollably.

I had to come to terms with the fact that she had loved me the best she knew how. I can only assume she loved me the way she'd been loved. I now know that some people will never be able to love you how you want to be loved. They can give only what they're equipped to give. I wish I'd known that as a teenager.

This is important for you to understand, too. Otherwise, you will be forever frustrated when some loved ones can't give you what you need in terms of love and comfort. It took me more than twenty years to learn this one. I was the unfortunate target. Being aware of this was a game changer.

When my grandma was still living in her house but in the early stages of Alzheimer's, I was lying next to her on the bed. "You are the one," she said. "I always loved you." I started sobbing and am doing the same now as I write this. I needed to hear that. I'd really needed to hear that, in that loving tone, years ago. Better late than never. It provided me some long-lost comfort, and it went a long way. It finally stopped me from thinking that I wasn't good enough and that I couldn't make her proud of me.

Understanding that we were from different generations with different mind-sets allowed me to acknowledge why she was the way she was. At that point in the mausoleum, I was able to forgive her.

I'd always heard that forgiveness had this power, but I was so deep in my own bitterness that I couldn't see past it. I still have a few more people to forgive. It's easier each time because I now know that forgiveness doesn't make what they did to me OK. It's not about forgetting or letting them off the hook. I used to think this, and those thoughts prevented me from forgiving. In the end, I realized that forgiveness was for *me* to move forward, to feel again, and to feel positive emotions on a regular basis and more often than negative feelings. And I finally am.

My dad is on the list of people I still need to forgive. When we were growing up, he lived three hours away, but we would see him a few times a year. We were never that close, but we had no hard feelings. That changed when I was applying to colleges. I called him and asked if he would write a letter to the school I chose, explaining my situation. My goal with the letter was to get extra financial aid because I had nobody helping me pay for tuition. He refused. I clarified that I wasn't asking for money; I simply wanted a letter.

At that point, only one of my five siblings had gone to college, and she dropped out after the first semester. I thought my dad would be proud to have his youngest child entering college. He refused to help. As I've said a few times before, when you hear something long enough, you start to believe it. Thus, I believed I wasn't worth even a letter. He's next on my forgiveness list.

I'm sure you have people to forgive. Whether it's for something big or for something small, it's worth doing.

I'm 100 percent confident that you need to forgive yourself. This is typically not a one-time thing. You will need to do this over and over. I know I did.

I wish I'd kept a tally of how many times I've had to forgive myself for being a jerk, selfish, mean, and too hard on myself; destroying myself mentally;

being too giving; not being willing to receive anything from others; putting up too big a wall; not recognizing and dealing with things sooner; letting things get too out of hand for too long; placing unrealistic expectations on myself and others; taking everything too personally; pushing people away too easily; not being vulnerable; not being gentle with myself; not forgiving sooner; not giving myself any wiggle room on anything; judging others too quickly; embarrassing others; not being able to accept compliments; using sarcasm and humor to deflect kind comments; not dealing with my stuff sooner; and trying to do everything by myself.

I think you get the idea!

I firmly believe that forgiveness may be the single most important gift you ever give to yourself.

Your Turn

1. Whom do you need to forgive to let go of your negative feelings? When do you plan on doing this? Set a time frame so that you don't chicken out.

    Who? _____

    When? _____

    Where? _____

2. How do you think forgiving this person will benefit *you*?

    _____

    _____

    _____

3. What do you have to forgive yourself for?

    _____

    _____

    _____

CHAPTER 10

My Enemy, My Hero

• • •

THE COOL THING ABOUT LIFE is that you constantly get to evolve, update, and improve how you see things. Your perspective is a continuous work in progress.

I have evolved on many things. In addition to talking about my problems and forgiving, one of the most significant and life-changing evolutions has been my relationship with vulnerability.

At times early in my counseling, my counselor would say the word *vulnerable* and talk about how I needed to be more vulnerable. My reaction was visceral. I would get flushed, start sweating and tingling all over, get fidgety in my seat, and want to slap her across the face. Violence is not the answer.

The dictionary defines *vulnerable* as "capable of being physically or emotionally wounded; open to attack or damage."

Seriously, vulnerability had not worked well for me up to this point. Every time I was vulnerable, I got hurt—and hurt hard! This is why I pushed people away and built a wall around myself. If I didn't let them close, I couldn't get hurt anymore. I was brilliant.

And now my counselor wanted me to be vulnerable? So did she want me to get hurt again? Maybe she was a bad counselor. And I was paying her for this?

I was so resistant and defensive. We even stopped saying the actual word *vulnerable* and started saying "the V word" just to ease into it. My wounds ran deep.

Then, as with most things, with time, practice, and a new filter, I was able to evolve. The same is true for you. I don't remember an exact watershed moment when I realized that vulnerability was cool and a necessity. I can't believe I actually feel this way now. If you only knew me way back when. But I eventually came to realize that being vulnerable is the key to happiness, connection, and creating change.

I do remember the first time I was vulnerable during my presentation to students. And I mean vulnerable about the molestation; it's my deepest, darkest secret. I had the most shame around that, and then I shared it with hundreds of people. I never thought I would do that.

This was a huge deal for me. I remember when I had my first counseling appointment and told my counselor about being molested. I was thinking, "Whew. I can't believe I just got that out. I never have to speak those words again. Ever."

During the assembly when I presented to the students—lo and behold— the walls didn't crumble, and the world didn't end. The students' reaction, however, was amazing. Yes, my sense of humor and method of sharing my story are big contributing factors. And my experience as a teacher is a tremendous advantage. But adding a deep layer of vulnerability has truly been the secret sauce to helping others.

Being vulnerable is not a weakness, as I used to think. It is actually a bold statement of courage and bravery. Whenever you find yourself summoning the nerve to say or do something, you're inherently being vulnerable.

I'm sure you've felt vulnerable before. Sometimes it turned out great, and sometimes it didn't.

* *Have you ever let someone know that you liked him or her?* Did that person reciprocate? Congrats! Did he or she shoot you down without hesitation? Sorry, it happens to the best of us and feels yucky. That's being brave and vulnerable.
* *Have you ever tried out for a team or school play or competed for first chair in orchestra?* Did you make it and succeed? Bam! Did you get cut or get put down as you were getting cut? Ugh, my heart goes out to you. That's being brave and vulnerable.

Let's focus on the latter part of both of these scenarios—that is, when you put yourself out there, and it turns out worse than you expected. As humans, we don't particularly care for getting hurt. As a result, when we do get hurt, we put mechanisms in place that will protect us for the next time.

Maybe next time you'll think things over longer instead of just going for it. I call that *paralysis by analysis*. You overthink it to death and never act on it again. If you do act on it and it turns out yucky, you go on autopilot to cope by using humor to deflect the hurt, acting apathetic as if you didn't even care in the first place, or tearing the other person down because if you're getting hurt, so is he or she. An eye for an eye.

I came very late to the being-OK-with-vulnerability game. I still get hurt sometimes. It stinks. But I have also learned that true growth comes from putting yourself out there, especially if you get rejected or hurt, because that's where you learn to bounce back and be resilient. Some of the hurts are small, and some are big. Either way, you can learn and grow emotionally and mentally from these times, if you choose. It is always *your* choice.

One of my newest ways to be vulnerable may seem silly, but it's been very challenging for me and very necessary for growth.

Historically, I'm terrible at accepting compliments and receiving kind words from others. Being hurt for so long with wounds so deep, I always thought that strings were attached if someone wanted to be nice to me. It was painful for me to accept a compliment. I was wary of an ulterior motive and assumed I'd end up getting hurt soon enough. That's been my experience. As a result, I became very good at deflecting the compliment with sarcastic humor, or I would turn the focus back on the other person. "Enough about me; let's hear more about you." I became a very good listener, because the more I listened, the less I had to share anything about me, which would be too personal. If I let someone in, he or she would simply end up hurting me. That was my survival mechanism for a long time.

As of this writing, I now feel rude if I don't genuinely accept a compliment or kindness. I don't like it when someone turns away one of my compliments, so I try to keep that in mind when I'm on the other side. I'm a work in progress. Growth and improvement take time.

From my experience, being vulnerable with my audiences has been so scary and so amazingly freeing! It has also given them permission to be honest and vulnerable in their own lives. That's empowering for them, and that's why I love my job. I never want people, especially young people, to feel as bad and as alone as I felt for a good chunk of my life. I want them to know there is always hope. Sometimes you just have to look a little bit harder to see it.

As I share my story with youth across the country, I am more vulnerable than I ever imagined I would be. Had I known how vulnerable I would have to be to live my dream career, I would have said, "No, thanks." I never would have pursued it. It would have seemed way too daunting and terrifying.

It didn't happen overnight. It was little by little, baby step after baby step. I can't imagine ever going back to how I used to be, so closed off to so many people and experiences. I was hurting so much. Vulnerability has helped me personally, and it has helped me help today's youth. By my helping them, they are actually helping me.

Vulnerability eliminates embarrassment, guilt, and shame and provides happiness, peace, and freedom. It's *always* your choice! It's a *great* choice!

The truth is, we hear what we need to hear when we need to hear it. Think about it. Your parents keep telling you to fill out those college applications before it's too late. You ignore them, because you don't want them telling you what to do. But when your coach tells you the same thing, you get on it right away. Your parents think, "Um, we've been telling you that for two months. Coach tells you once, and you do it?"

It's the same message but a different messenger. The same is true for your experience with this book. I'm confident you will take something productive from it that you will apply to your life to make it better. If you come back in one year and read it again, you will likely find something new that you can take with you, because your life will not be exactly the same next year.

Your Turn

1. What is one thing you have wanted to do but were afraid to because you have to be vulnerable?

   _____

   _____

   _____

2. How do you think you would benefit from acting on that thing in the previous question, regardless of the outcome?

   _____

   _____

   _____

3. What is the most vulnerable/brave thing you have ever done? How did it turn out?

   _____

   _____

   _____

CHAPTER 11

Let's Wrap It Up

• • •

CONGRATULATIONS ON REACHING THE END of the book. I'm proud of you!

This is the last chapter. I'm using it to bring it all together, a "What does it all mean?" and "What do I do now?" chapter.

I'm not going to be too concerned about winning the Pulitzer Prize or doing poetic justice in this chapter. I'm going rapid-fire because it's not how you start; it's how you finish.

May I suggest that you star a few items below that speak directly to you right now. Then come back to this page periodically and mark different (or the same) items that speak to you at those moments in time. It's like a checklist of mottos or mantras.

In no particular order, here's what I know for sure (Oprah reference):

* If it matters to you, it matters.
* Some people will always be awesome and helpful.
* Some people will always be selfish jerks.
* When they are jerks, it's rarely about you.
* Stop taking everything so personally.
* Go to counseling (or have someone to talk to).

- Stop comparing.
- Laugh more.
- Cry more.
- Showing your emotions is normal and healthy.
- Perfection is not a human quality.
- Mistakes are the best teachers.
- Stop blaming others.
- Stop giving away your power.
- Life is not fair.
- Stop acting like a victim (even if you are one).
- Make your pity party quick, and then move on.
- Struggles are huge contributors to your awesomeness.
- Surround yourself with quality people.
- Forgiveness works.
- Laugh at yourself.
- Vulnerability is transformative.
- Take action.
- Don't let people put you in a box.
- Keep moving forward.
- Punch fear in the face.
- Be kind.
- Be different.
- Ask questions.
- Listen more.
- Look people in their eyes.
- Work hard.
- Don't cut corners.
- Everything is possible.
- There is always hope.
- Stop making excuses.
- Have a head-underwater moment (have many).
- Say what you mean; mean what you say.

* Be on time.
* Believe in yourself.
* Let people help you.
* Flip your 20.
* Choose your filter.
* Get back up.
* Take control of your mind-set; take charge of your life.
* You have the right to be happy.
* You deserve to be loved.
* You are valuable.
* You matter.

Appendix

• • •

MY PRIVATE E-MAILS

WELL, MY FRIEND, THANK YOU for allowing me to be a part of your journey to greatness. Now that we're friends, I want to share some of my private e-mails that I sent to my friends after accomplishing two of my biggest goals.

I have done very little editing on purpose. I wanted to keep it authentic to how I had originally sent them. I hope they inspire you, make you laugh, and ignite a spark to have you go after your goals. Enjoy!

E-mail #1

Howdy Everybody! I hope this e-mail finds you all healthy and happy! This is the recap of my latest goal...and I didn't proof-read...no really...I didn't. Hope it makes sense. And since I don't do Facebook, use your imagination and pretend this is on my wall, page, or post...whatever you kids call that fancy technological stuff. :-) On Sunday, I participated in the Ironman Syracuse 70.3 (1/2 Ironman). It consists of a 1.2-mile swim, 56-mile bike, and half marathon (13.1 miles). After five months of official training, the day finally arrived. The weather looked perfect. Cool in the morning, forty-six degrees at 5:00 a.m. with a high of seventy, clear skies, light wind. My main goal was to just finish within the eight-and-a-half hour time limit. I had no intention of making the same mistake of having a set time goal like I did back during my marathon years. (Three marathons in three consecutive summers, all on a broken foot.) Just finish! As I set up in transition before the swim, I notice all of the spectators in winter hats, scarves, jackets, and so forth. And I'm thinking, I still have to get into the water and I can definitely see my breath. Did I say "perfect" weather? Anywho, I have thirty minutes from the time the pros begin until my wave. No...I chose not to participate in the pro category this time. I thought it would be nice to let somebody else take the prize money for a change. I'm thoughtful like that.

I finally get my wetsuit on and hand over my "morning clothes" bag to the tent. For the first time my feet are bare and the grass if freezing and I can't feel my feet. They go numb instantly. Again... perfect. No feeling is status quo until it's time to get in the water, in which case they defrost a bit. The sun just started to come up and there was a light fog coming off the very calm water. It was beautiful! My wave starts and the water is cold on my face, but I stay focused and hope to be out in fifty minutes. All is going well, even with the guys from the waves behind me passing me...this was to be expected. I felt good and got into my rhythm as much as possible, but every few minutes I'd be in a bunch of congestion. Open-water swimming is a full-contact sport.

At one point I felt like I was in an SNL skit for the Roxbury Guys. Two people sandwiched me and smashed me back and forth for a few strokes. But I really knew it would be a good day when I noticed that I do a good job swimming in a straight line. Saves a lot of time and energy. I cannot say the same for the totally an-noying lady who kept zigzagging right in front of me and cutting me off...over and over and over and over. Finally, I just stopped and said out loud (but not *really* loud enough for her to hear), "Oh

My God! Pick a straight line and stay with it. You are so annoying right now!" Then I continued on and started laughing at myself. I knew it would be a good day if I could tell someone off and then continue in my own peaceful head as if nothing had happened.

I leave the water in fifty-five minutes. I'm happy! It was still cold so I put on an extra layer and a headband to keep my sensitive ears warm. Wore them the whole way. Miles two to eleven are basically uphill. I rode the course in July so at least I knew there were no surprises. My left knee acted up a little bit, but I knew it wouldn't affect my run, so it was a no-brainer "suck it up" kind of thing.

The other racers were super supportive. Everybody was complimenting everybody along the way. It was a pretty cool thing to see/hear. It felt kind of good seeing other people go really slow up the hills, too. Training by myself the whole time, I didn't really have any other reference points. So I guess what I'm saying is that it felt good to see people struggle. I am like the most compassionate person in the world. :-)

There is this one hill I call the manic-depressive hill. I thought it was at mile forty, but all of a sudden I realize it's right in front of me at mile twenty. Good thing there was no time to prepare. Just do it! I gave it this name because you are careening down at forty-one mph (manic) and then in the blink of an eye you are climbing at five mph (depressing). The good part about the manic part is that my first skydive experience this summer helped a lot with my fear of the downhill speed. Once you jump out of an airplane and plummet toward the earth at 120 mph in free fall, 40 mph on a bike doesn't really seem like a big deal anymore. It's all in your perspective.

I'm always impressed by these tall triathlete-body guys and girls. They look so amazing whipping by me with their long levers churning their pedals. I wonder if when they pass me and my short legs (seriously, I tried on capri pants once and they were the same length as my regular pants), they want to ask me if I borrowed my bike from the monkey who "performs" at the circus… rides a little baby tricycle…isn't that where the "tri" part of this race came from?

One of the most unique parts of the bike was my stop at a porta-potty on the bike. Don't worry, I won't get gross here…continue reading. I come out of the bathroom and exclaim, "These are the most amazing porta-potties I have ever been in!" All of a sudden, a lady comes running across the street and asks if I can say that on camera so she can put it on their town website. So I say sure…it's not like I had anything better to do. Why not oblige this excited lady with a video camera with a thirty-second testimonial about the portable poopers! I must say, they were all meticulously clean, had a beautiful fresh scent, were decorated with orange-and-blue flowers, and had a triathlon picture in each one, a garbage can, and a floor mat/rug. Seriously, they were wicked nice!

After my interview with *Entertainment Tonight*, I finished my bike ride in three hours and forty-five minutes. Made another potty stop and got ready for my run. I delayered and was ready for the final event. There was a ton of shade, and I never really felt too hot. The people at the aid stations were super fun and encouraging, too. There are two loops with a little out and back on the front and back ends. On my first loop, I really wanted to be on my second loop. I really just wanted to head back to the park and be a finisher. I decided to stop whining to myself and just focus on running a great lap.

Then part of my right quad started to cramp up. UGH! This has happened during my marathon and long runs before. It hasn't happened for a long time, but I knew this could be a disaster and it started about two and a half miles in! I decided to just run through it and see if it would work itself out or seize up and be agonizing. After another couple of miles it went away…and never came back. :-) I had a great first lap and began my second. I felt great physically…I actually had a spring in my step…not how I would ever characterize my running form. Mentally, I felt solid, too.

Then without warning, my emotions started to take over. My eyes started welling up with tears, and my nose and throat got a bit plugged. I didn't realize how emotional this whole journey would be. But I was reflecting about the past five months of training and what it would feel like to cross the finish line, and I was overcome with emotion. This caught me off guard and caused me to walk to regain my composure. Problem being…it kept happening for like the last four to five miles! I had a much slower second lap because I had to do a run/walk. It was bizarre. I really felt great physically, and there was no reason to walk as much as I did…I just couldn't get my emotions together. My choices were to not think at all or only focus on one step (literally) at a time. Neither of these are particularly good options for me. Good thing is, I knew I was going to finish in the allotted time and didn't feel that pressure, so I just kept moving forward.

When all is said and done, seven Vanilla Bean GU packets, half a Cookies and Cream PowerBar, and tons of water later, I did cross the finish line in a time of 7:08.40. Interestingly enough, I did not cry then…but have a few times since. I struck a few cool poses for the photographer as I finished, got a free massage, got some food, and drove home.

Cool side note (as if this whole ridiculously long e-mail isn't a side note): I don't feel as sore and tight now as I did after I finished.

Monday and Tuesday will be the real test. As I crossed the finish line, I thought to myself, "Now what? What should be my next goal?"

Hhmmmm…uummmmm…let's see…well…how about on Sunday, September 9, 2012…Ironman Wisconsin! The full one, the whole thing…to officially be called an "Ironman."

Thanks for taking some time to read this. I hope you got a few smiles or chuckles out of it. But most of all, I hope it inspires you to achieve a goal you have always wanted to achieve. Whether it be big or small, as long as it's important to you, it matters. Go for it! Get 'er done!

Peace,

Pipes/Molly!

<u>E-mail #2</u>
Good Morning!

Yesterday on Sunday, 9/9/12, I competed in, um, participated in my first full Ironman Wisconsin (IMWI) in Madison. The event consists of a 2.4-mile swim in Lake Monona, a 112-mile bike ride out in the country, topped off with a full 26.2-mile marathon. Each athlete has seventeen hours to finish…7:00 a.m. to midnight. I was aiming for fourteen*ish* hours. Here's my rendition of what happened along the way…

**Oh, before you start: I did not proofread this and it is my longest one yet. It is very, very, very long. But I try to paint a picture for you because I know there are lots of questions. Hopefully, I will answer a bunch for you in this e-mail. I also hope you find it entertaining, inspiring, and of course funny. :-) And I apologize in advance if my thoughts jump around or aren't really coherent.

I have always wanted to do, or should I say "be" an Ironman since I was a lot younger. I remember watching it on TV, the Ironman championship held in Hawaii, and thinking, "That looks hard; I want to do that someday." As a lot of you know, I have been afraid of water most of my life and didn't know how to swim for a long time.

It all started when I signed up for IMWI last year on 9/12/11, the day after last year's race. It usually sells out quickly beginning at noon the next day. This year's race sold out in twenty-one hours. No turning back now—it's official, I'm doing it. I began my thirty-eight-week training program on 12/19/11. For the next nine months, I trained six days a week. Three-fourths of those days were double training (a.m. and p.m.) with Saturdays in the latter months being consecutive triple training sessions.

An "interesting twist" happened along the way…I lost my job… again…in the spring. Fortunately, my training kept me sane and sober while job hunting. I am fortunate to have had that to keep me positively focused throughout the job hunting process. I have secured another full-time teaching job. :-)

So I headed out to Madison on Thursday. I took my bike apart and packed it in a Thule bike box all by myself. I'm a big girl now. It was quite empowering to take a bike apart and put it back together again. I wish I had been there to help Humpty Dumpty. :-) When my bike came around at baggage claim, I had a good vibe that all would go according to plan. Just as I had visualized.

I stayed with my friends, Becky and Scott, which was awesome. They live about thirty minutes from the race site, and I didn't really want to be around downtown where all the other athletes were. You can get caught up in all that is happening down there, and I needed to be away from it when possible. My friend Beav was on his way up from Cincinnati, but sadly had car trouble and had to turn around. My other friend, Tricia, and her husband, Fab, visited on Saturday and also came to the race. It was great to know I would see familiar faces on the course out in Cheesehead land.

There's a lot to do in the two days prior to the race, so getting in and out, and being organized was huge. When I signed in, I was given this totally sweet Ironman transition bag (backpack). I have coveted this bag for many years, so when the volunteer gave it to me, it hit me like, "OMG, this is really happening…and I am now the owner of this bag." My heart dropped. Here we go…no turning back now.

I love to people watch. This kind of event is priceless. The bodies on some of these athletes are unreal. They are so fit and ripped, and embody what it means to be an endurance athlete. In addition, the beauty of this kind of event is that the competitors come in all shapes, sizes, and ages. As the Ironman motto says, "Anything is possible." The youngest competitor was eighteen and the oldest seventy-three.

Anywho…race-day forecast is virtually perfect. I'll explain the "virtually" part later. After a wicked hot summer, race day was forecast to be fifty in the morning with a high of seventy-one to seventy-two in the afternoon. Water temp at seventy-two. Then dropping to low sixties into the evening when I would be finishing the marathon. Couldn't have asked for a better day…almost.

At 4:00 a.m., the alarm goes off. I feel rested and have a big smile on my face because today is the day. Eat, bathroom ;-), pour some coffee, and I'm out the door by 4:45 a.m. On a side note, it's really amazing how beautiful the sky is and all the stars I could see since there aren't any street lights where they live. I wish I could see stars like that every night…or every morning before 5:00 a.m. Let's stick to every night—I'm not *that* crazy!

I drop of some bags I'll need on the bike and run courses, and head to transition to put water bottles on my bike. It's quite a sight to see twenty-four hundred athletes in the pitch-black (lighting was provided) tending to their bicycles like they are the most precious things on the earth. These people are a little out there. Of course, if my bike cost $10,000, I would treat it that way. Yes, some cost that much and more…not mine.

It's pretty quiet at this time: nervous energy, nervous GI tracts. ;-) The announcer is providing race info and positive words throughout. I made another bathroom visit. ;-) All is working well this morning. It's going to be a great day. From 6:30 a.m. to 7:00 a.m., the athletes don their wetsuits and head to the water. It took a full half hour to get everyone in the water. What a sight to behold with the sun coming up on calm water. Almost a thousand of the athletes were Ironman newbies. Can you imagine their internal dialogue just moments before the cannon goes off?

My thoughts…usually I'd be very emotional. I thought I'd have a good cry on the drive down or while waiting. But today was different: this was what I trained nine months for, and this was all going exactly as I had visualized it going. I wanted to be focused, so I was. I wanted to be calm, so I was. I wanted to be present in the moment, so I was. I wanted to appreciate the whole race-day experience, so I did.

At 6:50 a.m., the professionals start. I didn't want to show them up, so I went with the age-groupers this time. What can I say, I'm super considerate.

At 7:00 a.m., the start cannon goes off for the rest of us. What a sight to behold. It's the calm before the storm. From virtually silent to a feeding frenzy of swimming. Picture it: water like glass turns into what looks like a piranha-feeding frenzy. Open-water swims are a full-contact sport. Plan on being hit, kicked, swam over, and so forth. I started near the back because I'm slow and was fortunate to have found my own space after about ten minutes. I stuffed a gel packet in my wetsuit by my ankle to fuel halfway through. I meant to practice this during my training but kept forgetting. Typical rule is: "Nothing new on race day." That rule is always broken. It worked out well, so I felt better that I wasn't going to be starving for the last part of my swim. But of course a few interesting experiences happened along the way.

First was the guy who was unable to swim straight and chose the best part of the lake...right in front of me. OMG! I stopped, popped my head up, and said, "Dude, learn how to swim straight you stupid idiot." He didn't hear me, but I needed to get that out of my head so I could carry on business as usual.

Then some guy came up on me and decided to do an interpretive dance of "Save a horse; ride a triathlete" and climbed right on my back. Now, I know I'm single, but there's a time and place for everything. I popped up and bucked him off me. Then I thought, "How cool is it that I used to not even be able to put my face in the water without major anxiety? Now I'm able to be unfazed with the piggy back ride I just gave a fellow Ironman competitor."

Then perhaps my most favorite open-water swim experience of all time: I accidentally—seriously, it was an accident—gave some guy a prostate exam…twice! It just happened, and I was stunned and trying not to laugh at the same time. As all those thoughts are swirling in my head, it happened again! I stopped and let him move on. Whoever you are, sir, my sincerest apologies. I only play a doctor on TV. Like I said, it's a full-contact sport.

Then the Velcro on my neck was coming undone and chafing my neck. I finally hopped up over the front of a lifeguard's kayak without even thinking that I could have flipped him over (hey, it's all about me at this point) and fixed it, and then headed for the last couple of turns toward shore. You are allowed 2:20 to complete the swim. If you don't make that cutoff, your day is done! I was aiming for 1:30 (would be absolutely amazing) to 1:45 (more realistic). I got out at 1:48. I had my wetsuit stripped off me by the volunteers and was ready for leg number two.

I headed up the helix ramp and into transition one (T1). The volunteers in the entire race were absolutely amazing! I can't say that enough. So my helper was Fran. She got all my stuff out of my bag and packed it back up when I was done. The females and males have separate changing areas because public nudity is a no-no! I think that's a good rule for all times of our lives, not only at an Ironman. :-)

So while I'm applying sunscreen to my face, Fran is kind of hugging me to attach my race belt with the bib number. Then she basically put my long sleeve biking jersey on for me over my wet clothes from the swim. She put on my biking shoes while I was trying to get some calories in me. My friends found a great spot near my bike, and I was able to say hi to them and share the medical procedure I did in the water before the bike leg.

I stopped at the porta-john and almost wiped out because the bottom of my bike shoes are hard plastic and have the metal clip on the bottom. Not finishing due to a bathroom wipeout would have been devastating. But I caught myself in time.

Then DOWN the other helix ramp for my ride. It was still chilly, and I had my long sleeves and ear-warmer headband on. The bike leg goes like this: head out sixteen miles, do two forty mile loops, and head back the same sixteen miles. I get out about ten miles and my left groin feels a little sore. I'm like, "Seriously, this is not happening." Then I realized it was my near miss at the potty. So I decided to pretend it didn't hurt because I still had over a hundred miles to go. The mind is a powerful thing. It can hurt or help, depending on you. I needed it to help this day.

Of course, timing is everything. And just as I was putting my sore groin out of my mind, I quickly noticed my next distraction. Oh right…here's the part about the "virtually perfect" forecast… uuum…what is up WITH THE WIND? So. Much. Wind.

This was the only bad part of the forecast, but a big bad part. Now this course has lots of rolling hills. Big and small. A very fair, challenging course. Especially because Buffalo is so flat. I climb fine— not fast, but I finish the climb, unlike a couple of guys who walked their bike up the hill. Dude, get on your bike!

Anywho, there are lots of turns on this course, and one with a logical mind, such as myself, would think that at some point due to the turns, you would get a tailwind. One would not think that you would have a headwind that could break your spirits virtually the entire ride. The tailwind was so short-lived it was a cruel trick from the weather gods. My first fifty-six miles were right on track with my anticipated mph. Plus, the crowd support, especially on three almost consecutive long climbs, was amazing. The costumes/outfits/music/cowbells/cheering were unparalleled. It's been a long time since I have seen so many men wearing speedos out in the open, other than the old men at the aquatic center where I swim. These guys were hilarious! I really wanted to soak it all in, so I interacted whenever I could. Plus, they cheer harder for you when you do that.

I knew the climbs would have a cumulative effect on my antici-pated ride time, but I decided, "It is what it is." We all had to deal with the STUPID wind; it was important to stay positive and focused. No pity parties in an Ironman. It's an Ironman for a reason—it's difficult. It's not called the plastic man! I decided to make the most of it, not worrying about my time and just keeping moving forward. Did I mention how ANNOYING the headwind was almost the entire race no matter which direction you were headed in?

I had a nice bit of eye candy when the lead professional males passed me on their second loop, my first loop. One guy's legs were so long (and muscular and gorgeous) that I think his legs alone were taller than my five foot one and three-quarters of an inch frame. As one of the top five pros passed, he was being filmed by the camera crew on a motorcycle. Just as he passed, I'm in the background of the video.

As I start my second forty mile loop, I stop to grab two new water bottles and take off my long sleeve top. It's sunny and about 12:30

p.m. but still a comfy temperature with just my tank bike jersey. Gotta show off the guns, and don't want a farmer's tan. Don't judge…you know how vain I am! The good part of double loops is, you know what to expect. The bad part of double loops is, you know what to expect. I knew to expect the same OBNOXIOUS wind. And there it was at almost every turn.

Good news: my bike held up, no flat tires. Oh yeah, except for this one thing. I had the Trek bike mechanics double check my bike on Saturday. All was well except that one of my three bike cages was cracked. Totally no big deal at all. Didn't matter; it still held a bottle. Remember, the devil's in the details. The cage is metal. So if you have two metal pieces getting bumped around on EVERY little crack/bump in the road…that gets annoying real fast. I should have taped it up on Saturday. But I didn't. So for about forty of the first fifty-six miles, all I could hear was metal banging into metal. Mix that with the wind…good times. The worst part was the sound made it seem like my bike was falling apart and would self-combust in ten seconds. I think the people I passed and who passed me felt "sorry for that girl—her bike is about to break." When I got out of my long sleeve, I jerry-rigged the cage with a piece of tape from a used GU packet to try to fix it. It did the job. :-)

So on the second loop the fans are a bit sparse because they head into Madison to watch the run. So there wasn't much encouragement, or men in speedos, on the second loop. But those hills actually felt "easier" because there was no crowd making it seem like you needed encouragement to get to the top. I say easier…until both of my quads started to cramp up. I was like, either keep pedaling or cramp and fall off the bike in the middle of the hill. I took option A. I still had about thirty miles to go AND a marathon… no cramping allowed! They went away and never came back. :-)

So I realize that the end of the bike is near as my odometer hits 103 miles. Only single digits to go. Now, as well as through the entire ride, I take my remaining distance and relate it to distances of my training rides at home. Like, "Sweet, only fifty-two miles left. That's from my house out past NCCC, Shimshack's, and back. I do that all the time; surely I can do it now." That type of thought process definitely helped.

So I'm about five miles from bike to run transition (T2). I had to ask another rider if we went through this parking lot on the way out because I have no recollection of this part. He says yes and must be thinking, "Wow, that girl's having a rough day."

There is a slight downhill at this point with numerous cracks/gaps in the lot. As I am hitting every single one, just moments from getting off of my bike, I'm thinking, "This is not the place to get a flat." I am already planning on carrying it a couple of miles or riding the flat, rim be damned! The sheer jar to the body hitting these is ruthless. So I did what any sane person would do. I yelled the following at the cracks in the ground: "OMG! You need to knock it off right now! Are you for real going to give me a flat this close to the run? You need to stop it!" At this exact time, another athlete passes me and looks back like, "Wow, that girl's losing it."

So I finally get to the UPHILL helix ramp. I'm totally getting into the zone to figure out what gear I will need to get up. As I start up, I all of a sudden feel totally energized and cruise up the ramp. The fans are cheering, the volunteers are waiting for me to dismount the bike, and everyone is excited. My helper asks if I need anything from my bike before I go into T2. I take a few swigs of water and then tell her, "Feel free to burn the bike if you'd like." She got a good chuckle out of that. :-) I was so happy to be off the bike...

seven hours and fifty minutes after getting on it. Yes, you read those numbers correct. I was riding for a full work day.

I enter T2. The volunteers are cheering and awesome! Megan was my helper this time.

It's 5:00 p.m. and I'm finally starting the final leg of IMWI. I was SO happy to be running and not biking! It's only been in the past few years that I can say I don't hate running. It's taken a long time: three marathons later and many years. But running is more famil- iar to me than swimming and cycling nine to five. "Biking nine to five, what a way to lose your mind." I love Dolly Parton.

It was comfortable and felt great, especially with how hot the sum- mer has been. Remember the rule "Don't do anything new on race day?" Forget about it. I'm a few minutes into the run and hit the first aid station. I see what appears to be my holy grail…po- tato chips. I needed the sodium to prevent cramps, and I grabbed a huge handful. The funny part is, I really don't care for potato chips. But I was shoving them in my face like it was my first meal in days. I don't think I used any of my fuel products. I stuck with chips, oranges, and bananas. They worked great! No cramps. No full or sloshy belly on the run.

Now it's perfect weather, and since I was running around down- town Madison and UW, the wind was mostly blocked. I was feel- ing fantastic. I had seven hours left and knew I'd finish. My initial thought was five hours to do the run. After a long, tough bike, I wasn't sure if that was realistic, but finishing was an absolute cer- tainty. My first mile was 7:45…um, slow your roll, girl. That's way too fast! The fans were really enthusiastic on certain streets, the mood was high, and I couldn't believe how good I felt mentally, emotionally, and physically. I even stopped to dance a little to the music some of the college students were playing for us. It felt good to have some fun, even though I'm putting myself through this. The course is two 13.1 mile loops.

I got to run through Camp Randall where the Badger football games are played. That was cool. I walked here and there to make sure I didn't "bonk" or hit the wall. Then one of the cruelest parts of the day was upon me. I heard that it would happen like this, but I'm stubborn and wasn't quite convinced. Then it happened.

The halfway point of the marathon is maybe thirty yards from the finish line. You literally run down part of the finishing chute and as other people are finishing you make a complete U-turn and head back out for another 13.1 miles. For real! The bad news is I still had a couple of hours left. The good news is I wanted to get back there! I knew that every step would get me back to there and that time I'd be the one finishing. I had to stay within myself and stay present in the moment so I could continue and finish.

My friends had great spots along the way and saw me a bunch of times. I walked a bit more on the second loop. I started to get pretty tired around mile eighteen. I walked most of twenty to twenty-two. Part of that with my eyes closed. Walking felt great. Closing my eyes felt even better—just a little cat nap. I did walk "briskly" to not lose too much time. I even tried Olympic power walking arms. Yeah, NOPE! No extra energy to move my arms.

Mile twenty-two to the end I did a run-walk. Less than four miles to go is so manageable. No problem. Mile marker twenty-three, twenty-four, twenty-five. A few more steps, and I've less than a mile to go. The last two to three miles I could feel the emotions trying to creep in. I held them back. I learned from my first half Ironman to not start crying too far out on the run. It's really hard to run while you are choking on your snot. I'm just saying! Here comes the throat constriction. No! Here comes the reflection of nine months of training. No! Is that a tear? No! Stay focused and present in the moment. Stay here. Stay focused on the next step.

Finally, I make the last turn into the chute that so abruptly turned me away 13.1 miles ago. This was it. This was my time. OMG, this is about to happen. I get the crowd going to cheer me on. Then I see it. Another athlete just in front of me about to finish at about the same time as me. We passed each other a bunch of times; I know her pace. Decision time. Hold up and let her go through and I work the crowd...so she doesn't "ruin" my finishing picture. Just being honest here...get out of my picture, lady. But what if someone comes up behind me. Then they are "ruining" my picture at the finish line. Or I could speed up and go by her so fast that she won't be in my picture.

Hhmmm...I'm *kind of* competitive ssoooo...I totally blew by her and starting pumping my fists and "grunting" a little to let some emotion out. Then I'm about to hear what I've been waiting months to hear. THE Ironman announcer, Mike Reilly, says, "YOU are an IRONMAN!" So he calls out, "Here comes Molly Kennedy from Tonawanda, New York." At this point I am so excited...the finish is within seconds. I wanted to let out another "grunt" or "yes"... but instead, I yelled out a swear word. I know, I'm super classy. I finish and let out a huge AAHHHHHHH while "posing" for the cameraman. I officially cross the finish at fifteen hours, twenty-one minutes, and thirteen seconds.

Immediately after, each finisher gets a "catcher": literally someone who catches you after you cross the line. My guy comes up and says, "Are you OK?" I say I don't feel good and might throw up. I repeat that, as I'm now kicking myself for that last little "sprint" and burst out of raw emotion. I think it's going to result in regurgitation. A lady comes by and asks what I need. I repeat the puking part and say I need to sit or lie down.

My guy is still with me. He grabs me a water, and when he returns, here is what he sees: my face in my hands crying so hard and deeply that he probably was ready to call the EMTs over because it looked like I was having a grand mal seizure. I was shaking and sobbing that hard. Then he says, "Is this your first Ironman?" I said yes, and he could relate because he was in my shoes for his first finish last year. And then I started "grand mal seizuring" again. It was uncontrollable for a solid three to four minutes.

Then I got my composure and had my glamour shot taken. Good thing I'm a pro at that sort of stuff. I headed out the holding area to meet up with my friends, changed clothes, and we headed home. I was so glad to be in a car, even though my body/mind still was experiencing PTSD bike flashbacks.

I think I was a bit out of it due to the "Holy cow, did that just happen?" feeling. I had planned virtually meticulously for everything up to that finish line. I had a change of clothes and then I was out of plans/ideas/thoughts. I didn't know what to do now. I told my friend I was bummed that I didn't hear the announcer say "YOU are an Ironman." I'd waited so long. She said he did. He said, "For the first time YOU are an IRONMAN!" How did I miss that? Oh right, that was the exact time I was swearing. Etiquette class, here I come. :-) As the teacher, of course.

My friend fixed up some pasta, chips, and beer for me. We chatted for a little bit, and then I crashed. It was 1:00 a.m. I slept great, got up, ate (I was starving), and started the first of three sessions to complete this e-mail.

I flew home and a couple of friends surprised me at the airport before my grandpa picked me up…super cool! I get home, and as I'm driving down the street, I see that one of my neighbors must be celebrating a birthday or something. As I get closer, I realize that's my house and my front porch is decorated with balloons, signs, and a six pack. Also very cool!

So it's now about twenty-four hours (actually it's now Tuesday morning) after I officially claimed the title IRONMAN! My body feels pretty good considering what I did yesterday. I think tomorrow might be the pain day (so far just a bit sore). I am now coming down from feeling wired when I got home. And I have to work tomorrow.

So as I leave you, many, many, many minutes after you began to read this e-mail…here's my runoff of what I know for sure (my shout-out to Oprah):

* Anything is possible.
* If you believe, you will achieve.
* Mediocrity sucks.

While people have a fear of failure, more people have a fear of success because it's easy to give up and not try. It takes guts and risks to succeed, set a high standard, and do it again and again and again.

You have to start somewhere.

Fall on your face and get back up.

Figure it out.

If it matters to you, it's worth it.

Barriers are fictitious things we make up in our heads. They don't actually exist.

The power of the mind and the internal dialogue that happens up there will make or break you. You choose!

I hope you are all well. I wish you health and happiness. I hope this story will encourage you to chase whatever your dreams or goals are...big or small. It's ALWAYS worth it in the end.

ANYTHING IS POSSIBLE!

Peace,

Molly/Pipes! (a.k.a IRONMAN)

Acknowledgments

• • •

FOR A GOOD PART OF my life, I felt as if I were on my own, figuring things out to survive. Reflecting on how I got here (writing this book and having a successful speaking business), I realize that it was not a solo journey. It's a daunting task to remember and mention everybody who has helped me along the way. I am acknowledging a few here. If your name isn't here, know that it is in my heart.

My grandpa for helping me get my business off the ground and for being the one constant in my life. The past three years have been our best.

Becky and Scott Nelson, Bridget and Patrick Gould, and Mike (Beav) and Emily Mulcahey for still being friends with me during some of my darkest years. Thank you for your continued and unconditional support as I follow my dreams.

Kristi Scalzo for referring me to Allison Paull Clement.

Allison Paull Clement for calling me out on my crap on day one.

Josh Shipp for creating Youth Speaker University (YSU) and giving me the knowledge and skills to live my dream of helping young people.

Gretchen Cercone for believing in me before I did.

Sherry Brinser-Day for your honesty.

Former colleagues and students who always ask how business is going, being proud of me, and saying, "I can totally see you doing that. That's perfect for you!" This really means a lot to me.

Learn more at www.mollykennedyspeaks.com.

Follow on Instagram and Twitter: @flipyour20_

Follow on Facebook: Flip Your 20

Want to help students, parents, and educators
increase their performance and resilience?

Invite Molly to your next event!

Learn more at www.MollyKennedySpeaks.com

Made in the
USA
Monee, IL

15648297R00085